Gearing Up

Gearing Up

Leading your Kiwi business into the future

Darl Kolb
David Irving
Deborah Shepherd
Christine Woods

AUCKLAND
UNIVERSITY
PRESS

First published 2020
Auckland University Press
University of Auckland
Private Bag 92019
Auckland 1142
New Zealand
www.press.auckland.ac.nz

ISBN 978 1 86940 902 9

A catalogue record for this book is available from the
National Library of New Zealand

Internal design by Amy Tansell/WordsAlive
Illustrations by Tim Nolan/Blackant Mapping Solutions
Cover design by Kalee Jackson

Cover image: stock photo 37745270 © AlexKalina/123RF

Printed in China through Asia Pacific Offset

CONTENTS

ACKNOWLEDGEMENTS

What a difference 10 years makes – a lot has happened in the world since we wrote *Changing Gears: How to Take Your Kiwi Company from the Kitchen Table to the Board Room* (Auckland University Press, 2009). We felt that it was now time to reflect on and respond to the challenges facing owner-managed businesses in the present-day context as they prepare for the future.

Our first and foremost acknowledgement goes to the many hundreds of owner-managers who share their experiences – good and bad – with us, so that we continue to learn and grow, just as we encourage you to learn and grow. Your incredible business successes are the inspiration that has led us to write this (our second) book.

The key source of our interaction with owner-managers continues to be The Icehouse Owner Manager Programme (OMP). It is a learning journey that gives back so much to those of us involved in the programme. It is truly wonderful to be part of the facilitation team along with the many other facilitators, business panellists, mentors and presenters – too numerous to mention – who each bring immense knowledge and enthusiasm to The Icehouse programmes. A special thanks goes to Raewyn Goodwin and Liz Wotherspoon. We also thank and recognise Andy Hamilton, who has always been a great advocate for our work and for growing businesses in New Zealand.

In writing this volume, we have been very fortunate to have Vaughan Yarwood, who had worked with us at the University of Auckland Business School, take on the role of editor for the author team. His professionalism and courtesy were outstanding as he retained our intent while improving our words. Vaughan's considerable business insight and pleasurable disposition were the perfect match for this project. As such, he was a key member of the team of authors who, together with the patient publishers and editors at Auckland University Press, have made this volume possible.

Thanks to all!

Darl, David, Deb and Chris

PROLOGUE

LEADING YOUR KIWI BUSINESS INTO THE FUTURE

In 2009 we published *Changing Gears: How to Take Your Kiwi Business from the Kitchen Table to the Board Room* as a celebration of owner-managers and their contribution to New Zealand. That book served as a companion text for the Owner Manager Programme of The Icehouse, an organisation that has assisted almost a thousand New Zealand small and medium-sized enterprises (SMEs) in the 20 years since David Irving, one of our co-authors, co-founded it.

Much has changed in the decade following the publication of *Changing Gears*. Writing that volume during the Global Financial Crisis (GFC), we were keenly aware of the tentative nature of business success and the vulnerability of New Zealand businesses to the global economic environment. As we worked on this new book, the US stock market was at soaring heights but the global economic outlook was uncertain. Perversely, after years of the barriers to trade being systematically lowered, a radical nationalist and protectionist movement is now sweeping several of the world's large economies, resulting in widespread business uncertainty. As we go to press, we remind ourselves that business growth cycles are just that, cycles; they change, and they can change rapidly. Thus, we have written this book with an eye towards a future that, while far from predictable, is not without hope.

Since that first volume, everyone's lives have been transformed by the incredible technologies exemplified by the smartphone, which have led to a revolution in how business works, how customers interact with brands and how near-constant connectivity has come to characterise our day-to-day lives. Social media plays a growing role in every aspect of business, from recruiting talent to developing a productive culture and engaging with customers. Customers, in turn, are able to use these same technologies to seek alternative products and services from around the world. Entire industries have been disrupted, with revolutions in retail (Amazon and Alibaba), hospitality (Airbnb), transport (Uber), as well as the potential mega-distribution of block chain.

Automation, robotics, machine intelligence and the Internet of Things (IoT) have likewise challenged longstanding views of what humans are good for, and debate rages as to whether these new technologies will generate as many jobs as they displace. Small business is not immune to these seismic shifts. As robots and artificial intelligence (AI) become more accessible, your competitors will increasingly use them – even if you don't. And so-called 'big data' now offers a previously unheard of amount of information about consumers, in the process throwing up concerns about data security, privacy and the appropriate boundaries for public and private life.

Society itself has also 'changed gears'. A generation of socially aware and community-conscious consumers and employees care deeply about the environment, including issues of sustainability, consumption levels and the effects of global warming. We have witnessed the rise of social entrepreneurship – business designed to achieve social impact as well as turn a profit. We are rediscovering the fact that each generation has different views about what is important in life, including how to achieve life balance, find 'meaning' at work and make a difference in the world. Communities now expect more from businesses, not just in terms of creating jobs and donating to local clubs and causes but also in offering career pathways for youth, introducing family-friendly policies and providing continued employment for seniors. Diversity of all sorts and at all levels is becoming imperative in order to be competitive in a contemporary world.

What, then, hasn't changed over the past 10 years? First, our commitment to you, the owner-manager. The more time we spend with you, the more we are convinced that your role in our local, national and international economy is critical to the success of New Zealand – not only as a small economy but also as an increasingly dynamic society that is respected around the world. Our second observation is that achieving enduring success is as challenging as ever – if not more so. In a world of get-rich-quick start-ups, most businesses need to work hard for every customer, every sale and every dollar they earn. And small businesses have to do this without the advantages of scale. That doesn't mean that you are not up to it but there is always work to be done. Finally, we continue to believe that many owner-managed businesses in New Zealand will grow not by reacting to business as usual but by actively 'shaping' the markets they encounter. This has always been the case, and we think that the best is yet to come. Ultimately, we want to help you 'gear up' for the future you desire.

So, what is new in this book? Since we continue to work mostly with established businesses, this is not a 'how-to' book for start-ups but rather a guide and reference for growing businesses that are already off the ground. By 'growth' we don't necessarily mean growing in size but growing a better business, which may mean honing internal or customer-facing strategies, systems and practices. We still emphasise clarity of purpose and the central role that you, as a person, must necessarily play in your business. We have dropped some textbook elements, such as case studies, but have kept the exercises that prompt you to interact with the ideas we present. And we continue to illustrate our ideas with practical examples. We hope you enjoy the result.

1

We know you, and you matter

Owner-managers pay their own wages. This is one key thing that sets you apart from other managers and executives – who also have significant responsibilities but for *other people's money*. The fact that you are responsible for paying the wages of others may be a source of pride (and occasionally of pain) for you.

We believe that New Zealand owner-managers are the understated heroes of the New Zealand business landscape. And it is you, the owner-manager, that we address in this book. You might be thinking: But I'm no hero – but take another look. Small to medium-sized businesses (SMEs) make up a substantial proportion of the economy of most countries, including ours. You are essential to the success of our economy. And our goal is to help you and your business grow and develop. We start by outlining some of the distinct characteristics of owner-managers and owner-managed businesses, including their challenges as well as their opportunities. We then invite you to consider where you and your business are right now.

Ultimately, we are committed to making New Zealand's owner-managers more productive, more profitable and more personally aligned with what they want out of life.

As we reflect on many years of working with owner-managers, we find several key themes that make a real difference in owner-managed, family and (non-corporate) agricultural businesses. These are outlined below:

Know yourself

This is the starting point to growing a better business. If we blindly pursue a business that does not lead to the life we want for ourselves, or does not reflect who we want to be, then we waste both our potential and that of those around us, as well as constraining the company's ability to grow. Although it embodies age-old wisdom, 'knowing yourself' can still be the biggest challenge we face today. Indeed, most of us go through life without asking the hard questions; there are far too many business owners who really wanted to do something entirely different with their lives.

We suggest that you set aside time to reflect, both on your own and with a trusted partner or confidant; seek 360-degree feedback from your staff; listen to your family and friends (especially to their complaints about who you are becoming); and remain open to learning throughout your life.

Stay healthy

We are never going to do well in whatever we undertake unless we are in good health and physically capable of seizing – and enjoying – the opportunities that come our way. This requires us to recognise patterns in our body and in our disposition. Not every day is a great day – but having a lot of bad ones is a sure sign that things are not right.

There are many paths to good health but no quick fixes. Short-term changes will not give you long-term improvements in lifestyle and personal wellbeing. So, you must acknowledge the condition, work to discover the underlying cause(s) and, with the help of personal and professional advice, address the problem in a way that allows you to make the most of what life gives you and what you have worked hard to achieve.

Engage your people

Owner-managers do not escape the responsibility to lead. But leadership is not just about making speeches; rather, it is an inclusive process that takes place between you and your staff. They respond to your ideas, your expertise and your vision for the future, and you respond to their need and desire to see how they fit into that future. The result is engaged staff who enjoy working hard and wholeheartedly, and who collectively go about their job effectively.

A business cannot grow without delegation. Owner-managers cannot do it all – even though most think that no one else could possibly do it as well. The underlying premise of delegation is *trust*. Without trust, you will not be able to constrain your desire to micro-manage the person you delegated to perform a task. Your company cannot grow if you can't let go.

Understand family dynamics

Families in business present one of the most potentially difficult challenges – yet these can also be the most fulfilling. Many of the most successful firms in the world have been, or are still, owned by members of the founding family. Fortunately, there are also some multi-generational family businesses in New Zealand, some of whom we are proud to work with, and we hope to encourage many more entrepreneurs who want to build enduring legacies of excellence.

Family businesses need to establish principles or codes of conduct that serve as rules for those family members who are active in the business, and create forums that allow the wider family to be informed about it. Successful families also recognise the value that non-family members contribute to the performance of the firm. We would also like to note the increasing success of Māori enterprises; some owner-managed, others part of wider hapū/iwi ownership. These whānau-owned businesses contribute much to both the growing Māori economy and the wider New Zealand business landscape. For these enterprises, tikanga Māori informs the underlying purpose and values that in turn underpin commercial success.

There's money in muck

Living in our paradise, we sometimes imagine that the best businesses are located in pristine settings or are based on high-tech innovation. And, for sure, these are wonderful endeavours that should be celebrated.

But they are often based on romantic notions which can make it very tough to make a profitable return on capital. By contrast, every economy has service needs that few of us are keen to provide, and often that is where there is money to be made. One person's waste is another person's product. We know of many highly successful businesses that thrive on waste materials, or do the back-office jobs, the dirty jobs and the niche jobs that others don't want to do themselves.

Build a top team

Many owner-managers manage their relationships with their reports in a series of one-on-one interactions, in a hub-and-spoke fashion. But a growing company requires a small team of individuals working together as a senior management team; these are people that you have selected and charged with contributing collectively to the overall company performance as well as to their individual function. When your senior management team is well established – which will take time and perhaps professional facilitation – it will begin to share your sense of responsibility for day-to-day operations and strategic decisions. The team members will then know that they are important, and you will get the chance to sleep at night, comforted that you are not alone.

The focus of this book is to share lessons we have learnt over the years by listening to owner-managers.

Value outside advice

We have observed that many owner-managers make big decisions in the same way they make small decisions – by using a quick, solo, action-oriented approach and a 'just get on with it' attitude. This can be a disastrous way to make critical strategic decisions. Even the most experienced and knowledgeable owner-managers benefit from advice given from an outsider's perspective. Such independent advice can serve as a catalyst for action. It raises issues that you may be aware of and yet, on your own, would not have addressed. It can also reveal that you don't know what you don't know. We all have blind spots, and in the case of businesses these can represent a risk or a lost business opportunity. Sources of outside perspective, advice and wisdom are not limited to consultants but may include trusted peers (other owner-managers), professionals, such as your accountant, lawyer and banker and, when appropriate, independent advisors and/or external directors.

Embrace a changing world

These days there is little excuse for not getting the information you need to improve and grow your business. Knowledge is everywhere; we just have to know how to access it. Cynicism or suspicion about the way new technologies are hyped up should not blind us to their potential for both our business and our personal lives. For example, a few years ago our owner-managers sniggered at the mention of social networking sites but now many of them are keenly interested in how such technologies are affecting their business. Moreover, the world is getting smaller, with greater movement of people resulting in more diverse cultures living together. If we are to attract and maintain the best workforce for our collective future, we need to respect each other and build vibrant communities together.

Compete internationally

In order for New Zealand to increase its overall standard of living we must increase both the number and, importantly, the size of our companies to compete internationally. Distance from markets and the small size of our own domestic market make this mandatory. This is not a problem that will be solved simply by making our large organisations bigger. Rather, owners of small and medium-sized businesses need to understand what is required to take the next steps to grow their business. Not every company needs to grow – but if growth is your choice, then you should have the tools to make that happen. Even if your business is focused on our domestic market, your customers are influenced by international social and technological trends, prices and delivery options. We might say that customers are increasingly 'born global'.

Understand how to exit

As much as you may love your business, you probably don't want to become imprisoned by it. To avoid that fate, you need to know how to transition yourself from being a hands-on manager to being a hands-off owner. Put bluntly, if your company cannot operate without you in it, it is almost certainly worth a lot less than you think.

Ultimately you may choose to stay on as a founder/director of your company and appoint a suitable CEO and board to manage it into the future. Alternatively, you may decide to spread your financial risk so that your wealth is not solely in the business itself. Thus, you might sell all or part of your share in the company to invest elsewhere, including in other established ventures or start-ups – you may not be a saint, but New Zealand needs investment 'angels'.

What delights us as we work with owner-managers is their thirst to learn. Most are surprised to uncover this interest, often after mis-spent years in the formal education system. But once they start interacting with peers who share their challenges, they become fully engaged with the exchange of new knowledge and the new perspectives it brings.

Getting to know you – the owner-manager

What are some of the differences between you and the typical MBA-educated 'professional' manager? First and foremost, there are major differences in the amount and kinds of risk that owner-managers face, primarily because you're working with your own capital rather than other people's money. But there are some additional distinguishing characteristics worth mentioning:

- You are understated, and nearly always have a subdued view of yourself and your business. You rarely show signs of bravado, aloofness or elevated self-importance. Ironically, the richer you are the less pretentious you tend to be. Many wealthy owner-managers drive a ute to and from work.
- You care about more than short-term personal wealth and luxury. While the notion that New Zealand SME owners are selfishly uninter-

ested in growing their businesses once they have the '3 Bs' – Beemer, bach and boat – is not totally unfounded, it is largely overstated, at least in our experience with *growth-oriented* companies.

- You often feel alone in your business, knowing that no one understands it like you do. Your accountant prepares standard financial statements without showing any appreciation of your company's business model. Your lawyers may lack business savvy and you seldom have open, honest discussions with your bank manager. Your partner at home does her or his best to understand it but can easily tire of the tedious nature of day-to-day business problems. Coping on your own instils in you a certain resilience.

- You do more than merely 'get by', and may be highly successful despite any shortcomings of your business. Your vast and diverse experience has honed your street smarts and your innate ability to 'make a bob' or survive a scrap. You are also able to sense when things are not quite right and know what to do in most – if not all – circumstances.

- Although you are very business savvy, you seldom think conceptually about how you make money or about the business model that underpins your business. As a result, you may not be able to imagine new and different business arrangements that might be required as your firm grows.

- You rely on intuition, and will frequently decide what to do much faster than staff in bigger businesses. Once you get an idea or a solution in your head, you typically get on with it – usually telling your staff what's going to happen rather than asking for their opinions.

- You are generally comfortable in your own skin. You know who you are and recognise that your staff would not tolerate a phony or inauthentic leader.

- You are both generous and tight. You may be quite generous to a sick employee and his or her family, or to your local school, but you will watch your money very closely when it comes to discretionary expenditure, such as R&D (research and development) and professional development and training.

- You are generally loyal to your staff and expect loyalty in return. You may be especially loyal to those who were with you from the beginning. This, of course, makes it more difficult to fire under-performing mates or those who no longer fit in the current business.

- You are usually time-poor and not in good physical shape. This is often due to a low awareness of personal health needs, such as how to exercise, eat, drink and sleep well.
- Family matters often infiltrate your business. Ownership structures, sibling rivalry, discipline and fairness can all show up in the day-to-day life of the family-owned business, with or without family members being physically present. If they are on site, even more dimensions (and perceptions) of fairness come into play between family members and other employees.
- Finally, your management capability is limited – if only because you have not experienced best-practice standards or systems of management. Even if you are an excellent manager yourself, you may struggle to expand this capacity throughout the business. Hence, developing a business plan, achieving operational excellence, developing human resource practices, implementing marketing strategies and creating a senior leadership team represent major challenges for you. At some point, the lack of these practices will begin to have a real bearing on the ability of you and your firm to go forward.

Taken together, these characteristics of owner-managers should remind you how intertwined you and your business are. You may often feel that 'you are the business' or 'the business is your life'. Others around you may feel that way too. Of course, to a large extent this is true. There is undoubtedly a large overlap between you as owner-manager, your business and your life. However, each of these elements should have a 'life of its own'. Your business should be able to operate to some extent without you in it. Also, despite your great love for your business, you may wish to separate some parts of yourself from it, for example as mother or father, daughter or son, or a community member.

We recognise this competing and complementary intersection of interests and portray them as the key intersecting elements of the owner-manager's world.

The Three Circles model

We have found it most effective to express these key intersecting elements as three overlapping circles – the 'you' in Figure 1.1 is you, the owner-manager.

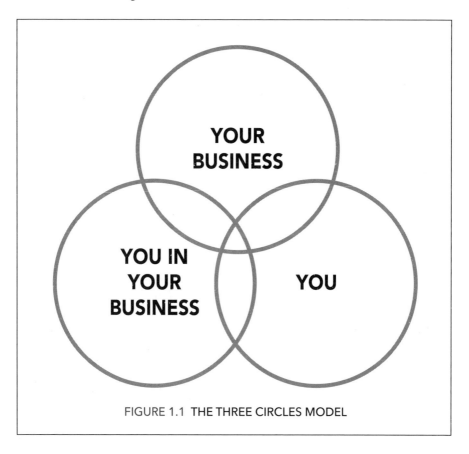

FIGURE 1.1 THE THREE CIRCLES MODEL

You probably focus a great deal on just one circle – 'Your business'. While this is good, at some point it will limit your capacity to manage 'You in your business', meaning your role(s) in the business. Likewise, you may seldom reflect on how *you*, your personal self, is doing. This is all quite natural, as the overwhelming demands of the business tend to squeeze out attention to other realities from your consciousness. Indeed, much of the support you have received so far – such as

There is a large overlap between you as owner-manager, your business and your life.

formal training, books and magazines, and even mentoring – probably focused primarily on 'Your business'. In this book we will address all three circles.

Let's take a look at each circle individually to understand their interdependence. The traditional circle is 'Your business', which includes such things as its purpose, values, competitive advantage, core competence, strategy, business model, and assets and liabilities. A business plan that describes the current state of the business and what it expects to achieve in the future should capture these aspects of 'Your business'.

In this book we will address all three circles.

'You in your business' describes the way you conduct yourself in the business. Typically you are the 'boss', which means that you direct, manage and lead the business. These roles address matters such as the organisation of functions, people, practices, communications, work processes, specific work programmes and projects, relationships with stakeholders and so on. Your role in the business may have been 'inherited' from your parents or from a former owner. It may reflect your unique approach to management, or it may just involve doing what you think you should be doing.

The good news is that you get to design your own organisation. The bad news is that it generally takes a lot of talented and experienced people to design an effective organisation, and you have . . . well, you have *you*. Basically, it comes down to designing your own boat – while sailing it. If only you could step off the boat and not be submerged in an overwhelming sea of matters large and small . . .

The 'You' circle is about just that: *you*. You may want to make a life, not just a living. Your desired life might be one that includes good health, a happy and fulfilling relationship with your life-partner, children and friends, and even some reflective time for yourself. This 'good life' is not independent of or counter to your business interests. In fact, if you are in good personal health and state of mind, you are better able to contribute to your business. In short, especially as an owner-manager, your health and wellbeing are essential for the three circles to function together.

We have been astounded by the enlightenment and power available to the owner-managers who get the 'You' circle right. You may not be a person who normally picks up magazines on healthy living but once you develop a reflective mindset, your interest in health and wellbeing is likely to increase. You may worry about: working too much and how you can better handle stress, changing your diet, developing an exercise regime. Even learning how to breathe properly can have dramatic effects on your energy levels, sleep patterns and overall mental attitude. These, along with minor changes in routine, can cumulatively translate to what is described as 'flow' – a great place to be, as we will discuss later.

A reflective mindset is helpful to health and wellbeing.

Throughout this book we will ask you to reflect on questions to help you understand an idea, concept or model by applying it to yourself and/or your business. First, reflecting on the Three Circles model, think about the issues that are facing you and your business right now.

EXERCISE 1.1 WHAT ARE YOUR KEY ISSUES?

List the important issues for:

You: _____

_____

Your business: _____

_____

You in your business: _____

_____

_____

In summary, the complexity of an owner-manager's life can be portrayed as the three overlapping circles we have described – 'You', 'Your business' and 'You in your business'. In a broader context, these circles also operate in relationship to family, friends and community.

Where are you now?

Regardless of the stage of your business, there are lessons to be learnt that will enable both you and your business to perform better. The focus of this book is on sharing lessons we have gleaned over the years by listening to owner-managers. It is about the challenges they face and the practices that help them to gain a new perspective on themselves, their businesses and the spaces in between.

Entrepreneurs seldom stop having ideas. Indeed, some move from one business opportunity to another; they are called 'serial entrepreneurs'. But this doesn't mean that they have been the same person in the same business over those years. As your business changes, so too should you change – otherwise your business would not be able to move forward.

EXERCISE 1.2 WHERE ARE YOU AND YOUR BUSINESS?

1. Businesses tend to evolve over time as they go from an inspired, impromptu, opportunistic start-up through unwieldy adolescence to a 'mature' stable business. Where is your business on the S-curve below?

   _____

2. Founder, owner, owner-manager, chief sales and marketer, holder of the culture and do-it-yourselfer are just a few of the hats you may wear or have worn over time. How has your role evolved with your business?

   _____
   _____
   _____

REJUVENATION

MIDDLE AGE

ADOLESCENT

START-UP

What keeps you awake at night?

One question we ask participants in our programmes is: What keeps you awake at night? We often discover that a high-revenue business may have lower-than-expected profit margins. The reason may be a lack of discipline or perhaps uncontrolled costs. However, in many cases it has nothing to do with gross margin, costs or even turnover. Rather, it may be the result of a deteriorating relationship with a co-founder, the co-founders or co-owners growing in different directions, or each party changing at a different pace. It may be the difficult conversation with siblings about how much of the parents' business belongs to those who work in the business and those who don't.

Many small businesses know how to make money but suffer from issues related to ownership structure and family dynamics.

Although we may not be able to address every response to this question, it is important that you think about it seriously and honestly identify the issues that may be holding you and/or your business back (including, in some cases, you!). No cunning business strategy or clever accounting practice can be an effective substitute for a difficult conversation. Once the big issues are addressed, strategy and planning usually become much simpler and easier to implement.

Sometimes what keeps us awake at night is not a big thing in itself but by operating in isolation we may have made a mountain out of a molehill. If that is the case, being honest about the small things that bother you will allow you to address them and move on to the more important issues in and around your business. One of the problems with isolation is a lack of perspective, so another of our aims is to offer you perspective on your business.

EXERCISE 1.3 WHAT KEEPS YOU AWAKE AT NIGHT?

_____

_____

_____

_____

Where to from here?

Successful owner-managers focus on the things that improve productivity *and* make their life easier. It is the old adage: work smarter, not harder. They focus on the internal success factors and build capability and sound practices into their business. You and your team could well be working hard but your efforts might not be reaping the corresponding rewards. Productivity requires more than just a hard-working manager or management team. It requires better systems, better talent management and a business model that delivers high-quality products and services. And this is not rocket science.

The remaining chapters address what it takes for you, the owner-manager, to become a more successful leader and manager of your business while at the same time enjoying a better life. For many of you, the challenges we have laid out will be significant. For others, this book may simply serve to reinforce the understanding and insights you already have regarding your business or businesses. In either case, our goal is to provoke you to think more deeply about what it takes to be successful and effective in your business and in your life.

To begin, consider the following questions:

- Where do I see myself and my business in 5 years' time?
- What would it take to make my company's employees a high-performing team?
- What will enable me to work *on* the business, not *in* the business?
- What can I do to improve my health and wellbeing?
- Can I really make more money *and* have a better life?

Hopefully, these and other questions have piqued your desire to read further. You may be the kind of reader who jumps ahead to see how it ends; that is fine. Feel free to skip around and read the book in any order you like. You may want to discuss what you read with others. We have provided a few blank pages for notes but you may also want to keep a separate notebook to remind yourself of key takeaways from your reading and discussions. Hopefully, along the way, you will find some insights that will help you become revitalised and happier as your business grows stronger.

Key lessons:

- You, as an owner-manager, are important – not just to your business but also to the economy and to society.
- Owner-managers are often isolated when it comes to training, advice and support; we hope that our ideas connect with you and your experience.
- We have found it important to address issues in three dimensions: 'You', 'Your business' and 'You in your business'.
- Businesses change over time, and change is a challenge for businesses of any size.
- Reflecting on what you are doing can lead to clarity about where you want to go and how to get there.

2

Grow what?

WHERE YOU ARE AND HOW YOU GOT THERE

When we talk about 'growth', we are not necessarily talking about making your business bigger. Sure, your company may be on a growth trajectory or even experiencing explosive expansion but for many small businesses, big is not always better. In fact, many firms we work with remain the same size but become more profitable. Or they transition from one generation to the next, which requires the owners – both old and new – to 'grow' personally in order to accommodate the necessary changes. However, before we talk about growth of any sort, it is important to understand your business as it stands today.

In his book *Good to Great*, Jim Collins urges us to 'confront the brutal truth, but don't lose faith'. We agree that sometimes we need to take a hard look at things and not be blinded by either optimism or denial. While owner-managers are renowned for straight talk and a no-nonsense style, they may nonetheless be blind to simple – but important – 'truths' about their business. Before any growth plan is possible, it is essential to figure out how the current business actually works – that is, how it makes money and where it might be losing money or failing to perform. This exercise is not for the faint of heart; it takes courage to confront the brutal truth. But without an honest stock-take, fancy strategies for the future are mere fantasies, unconnected with present realities. You cannot build a great business in the future without knowing how good – or bad – your current business is.

Many successful business owners struggle to identify exactly how they make money – that is to say, what their business model is. It is often a revelation when owners finally understand how key people, systems or processes that they thought were indispensable were actually costing them a great deal of money without clear benefit. We will address this issue later. Now, in order to develop a profile of your current business, we begin by asking you to take a fresh look at the business from a historical perspective. How does your company's history influence the business as it is today? What facets of that history can serve as a platform for future growth? And what aspects of it can you let go of in order to move forward?

How did I get here?

It's good to know where you want to go but it's also important to understand where you have come from. This might sound like old-fashioned advice but understanding the background and context of any business is a crucial step in determining how that business might grow and where it might go in the future. Exploring your past can be a generative source of inspiration for you and of pride for your staff. We know of owner-managers who have created historical photo displays in their company staffroom to give employees a feel for the history of the business. The 'good ol' days' may have been wonderful in hindsight – as well as extremely hard work. However, the ethic of serving customers – of being there for them no matter what – often comes through in the pictorial history of a business too, and that is something you can build on.

Exploring your past can be a source of inspiration and pride.

Paradoxically, as a business grows over time, the owner's role often changes and becomes somewhat more disconnected from day-to-day matters. Thus, making the company's history and values explicit helps others in the business pass them on. Storytelling has always been a powerful way to bring people along with us, whether we are fighting a battle, playing a sport or building a business. You may not consider yourself to be a storyteller but what you say, and the stories you tell, reveal a lot about you and your values. And when staff understand and buy into the values of a company, they need fewer rules and less direct supervision. We all need to 'make sense' of our world, and a clear understanding of your company's history and values can make a big difference in ways that matter, including fostering staff pride, encouraging practical problem-solving and increasing profitability.

Where you have come from

Founders do not merely leave behind resources and 'war stories'. They embed values into the business that often endure. When you dig out old photos, what do you see? What do those photos tell you about what and who was important then? Are these same people or things still important to you and your business? If so, why? And if not, why not? What has changed?

EXERCISE 2.1 REFLECT ON WHERE YOU HAVE COME FROM

Note the following for your business:
Founder(s):

_____

_____

Historical context:
List three things about the business environment that helped shape and drive the company in the early days, e.g. few competitors, one large established player, new technology with few providers.

1. _____
2. _____
3. _____

Founder's or founders' values:
List three core values that shaped the company's early years, e.g. hard work, frugality, passion for product, loyalty to customers.

1. _____
2. _____
3. _____

Key events:
List three critical events in the company's history, e.g. first sale to international customer, death of founder(s), establishment of first branch office or store.

1. _____
2. _____
3. _____

Who else matters?

If you are part of a family enterprise, you are not an island unto yourself. You may have a parent and/or siblings who own a majority share of it. You may have brothers, sisters, aunts, uncles or cousins on the payroll. Even if you are the only family member working directly in the business, you are representing the family's name and interests on a day-to-day basis. The business may even bear the family's name. In any case, your family's reputation may be closely related to the behaviour of the business. We will return to issues related to family businesses later in the book but suffice it to say here that when it comes to an owner-managed business, family matters.

Who else matters in your business? Well, of course, all your employees, your customers and your suppliers do. The web of relationships between these people is the essence of business, no matter what industry you are in. It is also where owner-managers can be the best – and the worst! Some have staff who would walk over hot coals for them, while others can't keep staff and therefore bear the cost of a revolving door of unmotivated workers arriving and departing. More often than not, even good people in a business work there *in spite of* the existing systems, not because those systems are good or reliable. And by systems we do not just mean HR (Human Resources) systems – although talent management is indeed a challenge, and an enormous opportunity, for most businesses of any size. We are also referring to financial reporting and inventory systems that make life easier for those working in your business, and induction and orientation systems that help newcomers understand 'how we do things around here' – that is to say, your company culture.

Founders do not merely leave behind resources and 'war stories'. They embed their foundation values into the business.

Living in a small country surrounded by ocean means that suppliers, distributors and logistical support all matter too – especially when the country also has a small population. In order to get business done, you have to get on with other businesses. This, too, can be a huge challenge for many owner-managers who historically have dominated a local, hometown niche and now have to share it with overseas and online competitors. Everywhere, supply chains that once were rock-solid are being shaken up as new technologies emerge and evolve.

What matters in this environment is the ability to work effectively with others. The challenge for many small businesses is not the 'tyranny of distance' but rather the 'tyranny of scale', in a world where the big just get bigger – and richer. This makes those on whom we depend all the more important.

In today's connected world, almost anyone can access or bypass your business. Customers not only expect to find you online, they also expect you to be active online, providing not just products or services but also expertise, advice and conversation. Your customers can brag about your business, or they can deride its service or product quality. They can lead new customers to you, or send them away, with the tap of a keyboard. Building relationships with customers online may be new and scary but it is vital. If you don't do it, your competitors surely will. You may be thinking 'not me', 'not my industry' but in our experience those who say such things are very often proved wrong.

Building relationships with customers online may be new and scary but it is vital. If you don't do it, your competitors surely will.

Finally, notwithstanding tweets to the contrary, we *do* live in a global village. Stakeholders of all types care about all sorts of issues that may seem very far removed from your local life. The people who care about social issues and the environment are the same people you hire or sell your goods and services to. One way or another, those people are your people. They expect you to care – if not quite as much as they do – about things that you didn't think mattered to your business.

Making sense of it all

If everyone and everything matters, what are the implications for you and your business? Do you need to find meaning to run a successful enterprise? Well, no – but it helps to know why you are in business and what matters most. You may find that deep down you are already fairly clear about why you are in business, who is important to that business and what makes the business work for others. Often, though, the problem is that *we* know what we are about but no one else does, because we are not that good at articulating it or discussing the meaning of (business) life. Sometimes, day-to-day activities keep us so busy that we don't have time to think about what it all means. Or it may be that the future is so daunting and uncertain that we would rather not look too far ahead for fear of being too frightened to go on.

Returning to Jim Collins' advice, we encourage you to confront the brutal truth without losing faith in the future. Our experience tells us that the more clarity you have about what matters most to you and your business, the easier it is to relay this to your partners, staff and customers. We also find that once you are clear about what is important, you can stop doing some less valuable stuff in order to do more beneficial stuff. This is good news for most of you who are currently taking on way too much in your business.

> The more clarity you have about what matters most to you and your business, the easier it is to relay this to partners, staff and customers.

To help you think about the meaning of your business, we have broken it down into the following key dimensions:

Purpose

What is the main reason your company exists? Believe it or not, this is not always an easy question to answer. You might think that every business exists to create wealth for its owner. However, while this might be true for many businesses, wealth generation is not the sole, or main, purpose for every business. For example, the owners of a family business may be more concerned with sustaining that business for future generations. In that case, short-term profit may be sacrificed or reduced in order to ensure the longevity of the going concern. Even a business that exists to make a profit often provides employment for the community in which it exists, and we hear owners express their sense of responsibility to provide work opportunities for others. Alternatively, a business activity may be used to support a social cause, with a portion of the profit being devoted to addressing the needs of others.

In his book *Start with Why*, Simon Sinek makes the compelling claim that employees and customers are increasingly first interested in *why* a company does what it does. Stakeholders first care about whether the company is a good one, and then consider what it does and how it does it. Millennials are far more drawn to companies whose purpose is to serve community needs – where 'community' can be local or global. Whether the undertakings are small or large matters less than the ambition of the enterprise to do good.

As you might imagine, the end to which work or an individual business is directed can have a huge impact on our feelings towards it. The more meaningful something is, the more intrinsic reward it brings us and the less extrinsic reward we expect from it. *Purpose* is the beginning of meaning in a business. Of course, almost all businesses exist for more than one reason. Profit and wealth generation are naturally part of the purpose of most of them but for many owners these elements are just part of the mix of meaningful drivers that get them up each day. Here, we would like to distinguish the 'why' of the owner from the 'why' of the business. If you were not the owner, why would or should your business carry on as a going concern? Think about the purpose of your business in its current form. Why does your company exist? It may have changed over the years. If so, how and why has it changed?

EXERCISE 2.2 WHAT IS YOUR COMPANY'S PURPOSE?

1. _____

2. _____

3. _____

Values

The effects of the founder's or founders' story and imprint, the key people who have played their part in the company's history, and the passion and purpose of the business culminate in your company's values. As with the other dimensions discussed here, values are not always self-evident or obvious to the outsider. Nor are your values necessarily the ones you have put on a wall poster. Values are what your staff will fight for, with or without you – or against you in some cases. As Mainfreight co-founder Bruce Plested says, 'If we asked our drivers to have dirty trucks, we would have a riot on our hands.'

Values-based organisations aim to align what is important to those working in the business (*individual values*) with the organisation's collective goals and aspirations (*corporate values*). Such alignment gives those organisations an advantage – it means that the rules of engagement make sense because they reflect what is important to everyone involved. As we mentioned, people like it when things make sense to them. Of course, the flip-side is that when attitudes and behaviours *don't* match the stated values of the organisation, individuals can become less motivated, cynical or even rebellious, because you are not 'walking the talk'.

Some people believe that values equate to competitive advantage. While this may be the case, commonly stated values such as 'honesty', 'integrity' and 'creativity' are really just table stakes, the normal minimum expectation of a business. Why would you even trade with an organisation that didn't exhibit those qualities? Google's motto may have been 'Don't be evil' but if your secret to success is not being a bad organisation, we think you can do better.

When you think about the values of your company, test yourself by asking: Would my employees agree? Would they come up with the same list?

EXERCISE 2.3 **WHAT ARE THE KEY VALUES OF YOUR BUSINESS?**

1. _____

2. _____

3. _____

People

What is the most important resource in the world? He tāngata, he tāngata, he tāngata (It is the people, it is the people, it is the people).

As this Māori proverb tells us, people are the essential resource in any endeavour. No matter the size or shape of your business, you need people to get things done. While purpose may be obscure and deeply buried within your company, you can easily see the people around you. Still, in our experience, many of you manage to ignore the people who make your business tick. Not in the sense of not knowing they are there – you probably count them every morning and make sure they arrive on time – but in terms of whether you really *see* the most important resource in your business.

No matter what technological tide is coming our way, the best offence is a culture and a workforce that are enabled to deliver excellent products and services.

Unfortunately, this is an issue that affects corporate warriors and owner-managers alike. As Tom Peters reminds us in his book *The Excellence Dividend*, no matter what technological tide is coming our way, the best offence (not defence) is a culture and a workforce that are geared up, engaged and enabled to deliver excellent products and services – something that, for the most part, robots still cannot do. Peters has long been an advocate of small players, in part because he dislikes behemoths that squander wealth and privilege and underperform comparatively, and in part because he sees SMEs delivering innovative products and services by empowering people to make a difference in the world.

As we write this, there is a near-universal fear of widespread job losses due to the rapid development and deployment of automation and artificial intelligence (which we address in later chapters). However, you know better than us that – even in a highly automated and augmented future workspace – your business simply cannot deliver unless you have the right people. The challenge for you and your business is to find, train and retain the talent necessary to remain competitive in a world that seems to prioritise people in business less and less.

EXERCISE 2.4 WHO ARE THE KEY PEOPLE IN YOUR COMPANY?

These are the people without whom your business could not operate as successfully. Who are they and what do they do?

1. _____

2. _____

3. _____

Passion

There was a book written in the 1970s whose title described New Zealanders as 'the passionless people'. Since then, the word *passion* has become a catch-cry for many Kiwis, who routinely use it to describe what they do – 'it's my passion'. Of course passion is a good thing but it's not the *only* reason to start a business, and it certainly is not sufficient to make a business work. A better word might be 'drive' – as in the determination to perfect a product or service through better design, higher quality or an improved business model. Drive is often associated with other cultures but we are now seeing more of it in the younger generation of New Zealanders who have grown up in a less certain, more pressured performance environment.

The key thing is that once you have a purpose, then passion, drive and commitment help make that intended purpose a reality. The problem is that passion can be misplaced or disguised within the day-to-day operations of a business – and, indeed, within day-to-day life in general. For example, being passionate about food can be a great reason to start a café but it could be a terrible impediment to getting the service level right in your wait staff. If you are more passionate about food than about people, you might not make it in the food business.

If you want to create a company that wows its staff and customers, then think about other sources and carriers of passion in your business.

EXERCISE 2.5 WHERE IS THE PASSION IN YOUR BUSINESS?

Who drives your business? Who has the passion? And passion for what?

1. _____

2. _____

3. _____

Other drivers – opportunity, service, calling

Passion is often associated with a good business but it is not a mandatory condition. Note that passion itself may be overrated in a small business. While it is difficult to imagine going to work in a field or an area in which you have no interest, some owners accept the fact that their business is not their passion. This doesn't mean that they can't build a great business. In fact, you might say that some people's passion or drive is towards building great businesses regardless of the industry they are in.

When owner-managers tell us how and why they came to their business, they offer a wide range of reasons. An opportunity may have presented itself and triggered the starting of a business. There may have been a 'lucky' discovery of a product or service that appealed at that point in their lives. It may have been the opportunity to take over a family business and make it their own. Perhaps while on an overseas trip they discovered a new market, product or service that matched their organisation's capability. Or a supply chain may have presented opportunities for consolidation, on which they capitalised. How much is down to luck and how much is about being prepared and attentive is debatable but the fact is that business success is often about seizing opportunities when they present themselves.

Increasingly, we encounter businesses that serve a social need. Of course, the not-for-profit sector has been around for a long time but hybrid forms are now appearing. These are businesses dedicated to a social need while still operating as for-profit organisations – for example, Eat My Lunch here in New Zealand. Globally, for-profit business platforms such as Uber and Airbnb see themselves as providing economic opportunities for drivers and home-owners as well as being efficient service alternatives for travellers. Why would so many people prefer to ride or stay with strangers? These businesses attribute part of their seemingly unlikely success to our basic social need and desire to connect with others, including 'strangers in strange lands'.

Passion is often associated with a good business but it is not a mandatory condition.

Whether for profit or not for profit, serving a social, technical or economic need is a compelling motive for running a business; for many enterprises, 'service' truly is the main reason for existing. Besides being the primary purpose of a business, service-as-driver offers many other benefits to an organisation. Clarity about whom you are serving allows others to buy into that vision. And it can become a substitute for bureaucratic rules and policies, where the service ethic becomes the answer to such procedural questions as: What is the right thing to do in this situation? If you know whom you are serving and why, you already know what should be done. Some might even explain their path towards helping others as a 'calling'. Indeed, your story might make it appear that everything you have done in your life has led you to do what you are doing now. Clarity of purpose is, of course, wonderful but being over-zealous can be off-putting for others and can blind you to other perspectives and approaches when you are addressing a problem. So, a service orientation is not a complete substitute for wisdom, advice and governance, which we will discuss later.

EXERCISE 2.6 WHAT ARE OTHER KEY DRIVERS OF YOUR BUSINESS?

1. _____

2. _____

3. _____

Growth for what reason?

There is more than one 'why' question in business. Why grow? Why change the way you are doing things? Again, we are not suggesting that every business must grow; but good businesses should embrace change, and this often comes through growth and development. Some businesses have a much clearer imperative – grow or die. If you don't need to get bigger but do need to improve, then that is also a good reason to grow your capacity to serve your customers better.

We are not suggesting that every business must grow but good businesses should embrace change, and this often comes through growth and development.

So, why do you want to grow? Are you extending the legacy of the founder? Are you building a bigger, better business on a solid platform? Are the foundations of your business being shaken by new technologies, new competitors or new business models? Do your people desire more growth in their work roles? Do they want to be part of something bigger and/or better – even if they aren't sure what that might look like? Or are you the visionary, the pioneer who feels the need to solve a massively important problem in your neighbourhood, community, nation or world?

Mundane as it may sound, we are happy if you just want to grow your profitability, your top line or your bottom line. You are probably going to meet some higher-order needs for yourself and others by just running a better business.

EXERCISE 2.7 HOW DO YOU SEE YOUR COMPANY'S GROWTH?

1. What is the key driver for growth in your business as it stands?

    _____

2. Can you describe your business as it will be in 3–5 years?

    _____

    _____

3. What part will you play to realise your vision of the future?

    _____

While we are intentionally focused on 'You in your business', we also encourage you to think about the business as it stands, without you. Your business has a place in the world in its own right. People lend money to it, people go there to work, customers buy from it, suppliers serve it and so on. Left in good condition, the going concern will outlive us.

We are asking a lot of questions in this chapter but we have found that unless you know *why* you are working on your business, almost nothing you do to improve it will be entirely effective. You may circle back to this list of questions and revise, change or update your answers as you work through the rest of the book (perhaps we should have told you to fill in the blanks with a pencil!) Of course, vision, values and opportunity, even knowledge of why you want to grow, are nothing without execution – a point we will continue to highlight throughout this book.

Key lessons:

- Knowing where you have come from helps you know where you are going.
- Purpose, values and passion are important but they are not the only drivers in business.
- Growth may be a worthy goal but it is not the only way to improve your business.
- Know your personal drivers but also think about the drivers within the business as an independent entity.

3

Earning the right to grow

While a grand purpose for your business is uplifting and motivating, it will have little chance of being realised unless the business has good 'bones'.

Questions relating to good business bones include: Does your business have the backbone for its mission? Can the business cope with the risk implied by its purpose? What are the financial numbers like? How timely is the knowledge provided by the company's information systems? What about your customers? Do they have a reason to continue buying your products and services at prices, and in quantities, that are profitable to you? And over what time horizon do you think about these questions?

Management consultancy McKinsey provides us with some context for that last question with its three 'Horizons of Growth':

- Horizon 1: Maintain and defend current value streams (50% to 70% of budget).
- Horizon 2: Develop the next competitive value streams (20% to 40% of budget).
- Horizon 3: Explore options for future competitive value streams (5% to 15% of budget).

In this chapter and the next we will concentrate on the near-term Horizons 1 and 2. These are periods in which we can see the future and anticipate what it holds for our company. Horizon 3 concerns subjects such as the future of work, which generates a great deal of both interest and uncertainty; we will have more to say on that testing subject in Chapter 9.

What are the numbers like?

Ever since The Icehouse began, owner-managers have heard us challenge the usefulness of financial statements prepared by accountants. In our view the mind of the public accountant is more attuned to the needs of the IRD than to what you, the business client, needs. The format of the statements he or she produces is the same for each and every client: total company sales less cost of goods sold equals gross profit, from which expenses are deducted to arrive at net profit. But does that explain where you made, or did not make, your profit? To know *that* you will first need to know the performance of the key categories of products or services, and what the sales and gross profits were for each of those categories. To be informative, the accountant needs to 'unwrap' the business.

To be informative, the accountant needs to 'unwrap' the business.

A question often asked but almost as frequently found impossible to answer is: What is the **break-even** for your company? In other words, how many products does the company have to produce to break even, making neither a profit nor a loss?

This question requires a deeper analysis of the business, and for that we need to understand the behaviour of costs – specifically whether or not a particular cost increases when more of a product is made and sold. A good example is the labour and material used to manufacture and sell the product – any increase in production volume increases the requirement for materials and people to produce and sell the product. In standard financial statements the element that gives the closest approximation to this is the cost of goods sold, which when deducted from sales gives the gross profit. Most of the numbers in the cost of goods sold are truly variable with volume. However, a better insight is gained by deducting all variable costs from sales to give what is called the 'contribution margin'. This is the key number in break-even analysis: in order for the company to break even, the contribution margin must equal the remainder of the costs, such as the owner-manager's salary, which by definition are the fixed costs. The question then is: How many units were sold to generate that contribution margin? That is your break-even point. This concept is often best understood when displayed in a graphical form, as in Figure 3.1.

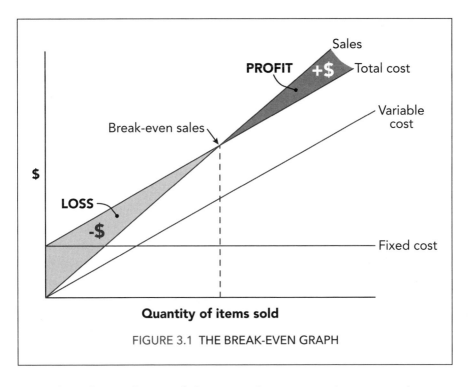

FIGURE 3.1 THE BREAK-EVEN GRAPH

Making the numbers work for you is always smart. A manager whom one of us worked for used simple algebra to make a very good business point. He cleverly turned

$$\text{Sales} - \text{Costs} = \text{Profit}$$
$$\text{into}$$
$$\text{Sales} - \text{Profit} = \text{Costs}$$

to make it clear that the business needed to make a profit in order to sustain itself. It elevated the importance of profit and shifted the meaning of costs, making them non-negotiable. In other words, once the owner decides that more profit must be made, then the business has no choice but to avoid paying higher wages or paying more for the purchase of goods and services.

Other standard financial statements include the balance sheet, the source and application of funds, and the cash flow statement. The last two usually serve the same purpose, though cash flow is the more frequently used – it is certainly the more galvanising!

As with all financial statements, reading a balance sheet requires you to know what to look for. The balance sheet focuses on the business's funding and how it is used. The general message is that long-term funds are provided by owners and long-term lenders, and these funds are applied to the purchase of long-term assets. Risk is the key determinant as to whether the long-term funds are sourced from owners or lenders. Short-term funds are applied to what are called current assets, and the difference between current assets and current liabilities (mainly short-term funds) is working capital. In the case of SMEs, short-term and long-term borrowings almost always come from trading banks.

Working capital is a key number. It is the money the business has readily to hand that meets the variable costs of running the business; for those of you who prefer gross profit thinking, a close proxy is the cost of goods amount. For current liabilities, key numbers are those for bank overdraft and creditors; within current assets, they are cash in the bank, debtors and stock. While debtors, creditors and stock are not cash per se, they are considered to be highly negotiable. For this reason a close eye is always kept on these near-cash items. So you will often see terms such as 'number of days sales tied up in stock'. The nature of the business will have an influence on this. For example, a food retailer may not want more than two weeks of sales in stock, whereas a food producer may require 1–2 months on hand. In respect of debtors or creditors, something like 4–6 weeks of cash tied up in debtors or creditors is considered normal.

A key measure of the overall health of a business is the **return on investment** (ROI). When looked at by both owners and lenders, *return on funds employed* (ROFE) is used instead. For the business owner this number is the ultimate test of whether his or her money is being used effectively. Given long-term interest rates of, say, 8 per cent, then safely meeting the interest cost on borrowed funds will require a return of at least 12 per cent on money invested in the business. As you can imagine, the ROI required will depend a great deal on the reliability of earnings. If the business deals largely in commodities, then a higher ROI will be required to cover the risk of being in the trough of a commodity cycle. On the other hand, utility products, such as petrol and electricity, have greater pricing certainty and therefore a lower ROI will be needed to cover the cost of money borrowed.

Banks protect themselves through **covenants**, which are financial targets that a client business must meet if it is to continue having access to, and use of, the bank's funds. The key measures are those that illustrate the ability of the business to repay the lender out of its assets, and earnings sufficient to meet the interest cost. Depending on the quality of the assets, the bank would want the value of assets to exceed bank borrowings by something like threefold. The earnings number that is used to measure the ability to pay interest is EBITDA (earnings before interest, tax, depreciation and amortisation) or free cash flow – and, again, this number will be at least threefold. Should a covenant be breached, the bank will intervene, and if the breach continues it will call in the loan. If played out, that would translate into receivership and liquidation.

> It is not a single risky investment that causes damage but an accumulation of risk investments.

For this reason, investment risk features heavily in the judgement of fund providers. Banks can often be ready providers to good businesses but overconfidence can lead to a breach of covenants brought about by those risky investments that don't perform reliably. Examples of risky investments include commodities, businesses expanding beyond their core knowledge, and investments that stretch a company's resources beyond its ability to manage. Often it is not a single risky investment that causes the damage but an accumulation of risk investments – though, of course, the size of an investment can play a part. The lesson is that projects with high risk require a greater proportion of equity finance, while low-risk projects can cope with a higher proportion of debt. Where more equity is required than the owner-manager can provide, he or she might consider bringing an aligned new equity partner into the business. After all, it is better to dilute ownership than risk the bank calling in its funds.

Almost every business that borrows from a trading bank is required to provide a **personal guarantee** (PG) to the bank. This raises a very serious question of rights. By their action the bank is seeking the security of your personal assets as well as those of the company. But the whole point of the principle of limited liability (as adopted by almost every company) is that the lender is 'limited' to accessing only those assets held by the company. In other words, assets not owned by the company – such as the family home – are not available to the lender.

In our view, owners do not sufficiently resist the banks by not agreeing to PGs. While PGs are hard to avoid, we know of occasions when the reputation of the owner-manager, as demonstrated by his or her track record, is sufficient for the bank to waive the PG requirement. All owner-managers should test the bank on this point at the time of borrowing; even if unsuccessful at that time, they should reach an agreement with the bank that provided certain earnings numbers (e.g. EBITDA) are achieved the PG will be waived. Needless to say, this position must be negotiated at the time of borrowing the money.

We have emphasised the need for good analysis with regard to earnings (so we know where the money is coming from), cash flow (so we understand day-to-day liquidity) and the strength of the balance sheet (so we will never have to deal with an angry banker). To do this, successful businesses use **key performance indicators** (KPIs). These are often financial measures but also extend to such factors as quality, operational performance and speed. A business should not be overwhelmed with KPIs but neither should it be starved of the information they provide – the number and range of KPIs should be tailored to the needs of the particular company. A typical series of KPIs might include measures of stock liquidity, creditors and debtors, delivery performance, quality, health and safety, staff productivity, waste and communication.

Are you strong and resilient?

In a business planning process, we ask managers to use three informative pieces of analysis to better understand the company's environment, its outlook and its competitive position:

- PESTLE analysis
- SWOT analysis
- Porter's Five Forces.

PESTLE analysis is a framework used by marketers to understand and monitor the macro-environmental factors that have an impact on an organisation. In the PESTLE diagram, see Figure 3.2, the letters stand for environmental factors, examples of which might include:

- **Political:** Political system, balance of power, layers of governance.
- **Economic:** Interest rates, inflation, availability of funds, terms of trade, labour skills.
- **Social:** Demographics, immigration, birth and death rates, income distribution, living conditions.
- **Technological:** R&D, innovation, digital capability.
- **Environmental:** Global warming, genetically modified organisms, resource management.
- **Legal:** Justice system, company, competition and labour law.

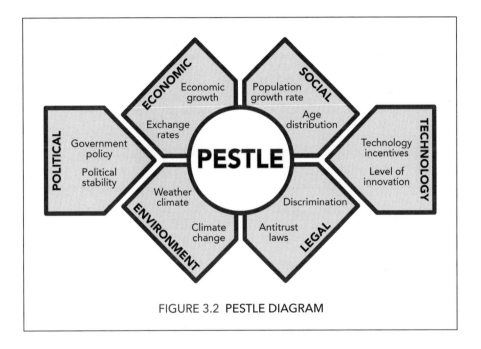

FIGURE 3.2 PESTLE DIAGRAM

The planning process involves going through each of these factors to test the extent to which the company is exposed to either good or bad conditions. Note that the analysis examines the *external* conditions – ones that are beyond the company's control but which if played out would affect it in such a way that they would determine whether a strategy is initiated or not.

The result of the analysis is then used to undertake a **SWOT analysis**, which tests the company's capability.

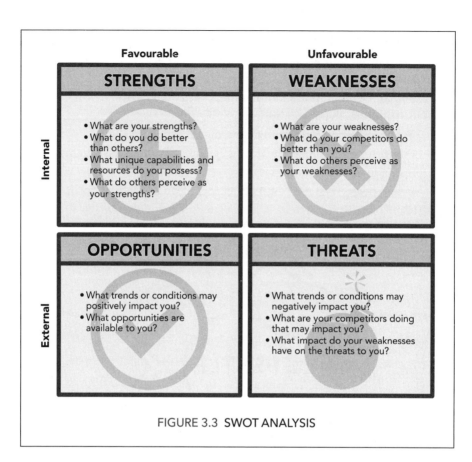

	Favourable	**Unfavourable**

Internal

STRENGTHS
- What are your strengths?
- What do you do better than others?
- What unique capabilities and resources do you possess?
- What do others perceive as your strengths?

WEAKNESSES
- What are your weaknesses?
- What do your competitors do better than you?
- What do others perceive as your weaknesses?

External

OPPORTUNITIES
- What trends or conditions may positively impact you?
- What opportunities are available to you?

THREATS
- What trends or conditions may negatively impact you?
- What are your competitors doing that may impact you?
- What impact do your weaknesses have on the threats to you?

FIGURE 3.3 SWOT ANALYSIS

As Figure 3.3 shows, the origin of factors is *internal* when analysing for strengths and weaknesses and *external* when analysing for opportunities and threats. With an objective mindset think through each of these four factors. Now understand how the company can protect itself from outside threats and take advantage of outside opportunities.

Porter's Five Forces framework, see Figure 3.4, completes the planning process by examining the company's position in the supply chain in relation to both suppliers and customers (buyers), and its competitive position with respect to substitute products and new entrants.

Analysis using Porter's Five Forces framework must be rigorous; nothing is served by under-estimating any of the parties involved, each one of which is looking to take from you: the customer puts pressure on price vs. service, the supplier puts pressure on cost vs.

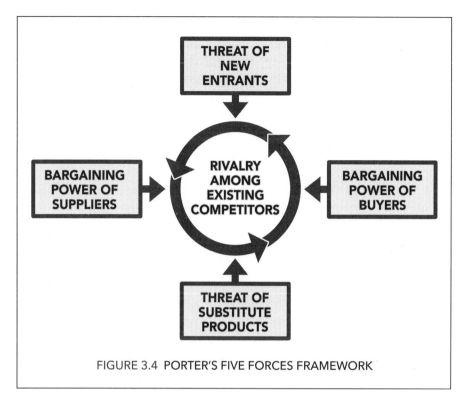

FIGURE 3.4 PORTER'S FIVE FORCES FRAMEWORK

service, and the competitor applies pressure by outperforming your company.

Every industry has its own characteristics and well-established positions in the supply chain. Think of the energy market, and we immediately have a picture of utilities with high capital expenditures and commodity pricing. For airlines the choice is either to offer full service, as Air New Zealand does, or low cost, which is the course followed by Jetstar – both of which are affected by the high cost of airport service charges. For food and wine it is about seasons, brands and large supermarket customers who are themselves increasingly being challenged by new online competitors. These days, no company or industry is free from the threat of disruption.

For our part, we have introduced the concept of **dependency** when thinking of the supply chain: dependency on your business by the supplier on one side and by the customer on the other. This is the ultimate basis for securing the highest margin by buying at the lowest price and selling at the highest price. Dependency advantage can derive from scale, brand, contract, uniqueness, capability or relationship. Not all of these are necessarily relevant – just the ones that operate in your industry and with your company's particular strategy. If you are competing in the mainstream, then least-cost supply will come from scale, and using your capability to find product differentiation will enable branding. In a niche market, skills and (hopefully) intellectual property will produce a uniqueness that, if sustained, will give you stability.

Armed with all this knowledge, it is now time to look more closely at what you can harness in order to compete successfully.

What are you good at?

Much of what we have considered so far concerns what your business is up against – customers, suppliers and competitors. It is now time to nail what you are good at and what you have to win with.

The analysis we use to discover a business's capability is grounded in **core competence**. The idea of 'core competencies', introduced by C. K. Prahalad and Gary Hamel in the 1990s, is a further development on competitiveness. When asked what their competitive advantage is, owner-managers will often use obvious, superficial explanations that relate to cost, speed, scale, brand and people. Core competence, however, is often far from obvious. It is deeply entrenched in the business and, hopefully, translates into a unique selling proposition for the company.

A core competency must be hard to copy, easy to replicate and add value for the customer.

A core competency must pass three tests: it must be hard to copy, easy to replicate and add value for the customer. Say this quickly and it does not sound difficult. But take the first test: What do you do in your company that is hard for others to copy? The question is not a usual one and clearly is difficult to answer. One possibility would be to have something that outsiders cannot see, let alone imagine. That would indeed be difficult to copy!

One veterinary business we know of had built a strong position based on the growing dairy industry. The key owners had complementary capabilities from which, unbeknownst to them, their core competence emerged. One owner was an epidemiologist with an insightful view of the state and the future of the rural veterinary sector, while the other was an equally astute business manager. This combination of capabilities positioned the business to take advantage of the trend towards bigger farms through either neighbour buyouts or corporate investment. These farm owners were a far cry from the typical shepherd-cum-dairy farmer. They wanted to engage in annual planning with quarterly updates and receive (among other things) a monthly financial statement with KPIs and explanations, a commentary on world dairy markets, sensitivity analysis for changing payout expectations, and recommendations on organic dairy farming. The two owner-managers in the veterinary business titled this expanded owner requirement 'complex farming solutions' and began to think of the implications using a completely different model from that of the conventional clinic. This was their core competence.

We find that owner-managers are most often very challenged when it comes to identifying their company's core competence. We can only say that rising to the challenge is worthwhile, as Figure 3.5 shows:

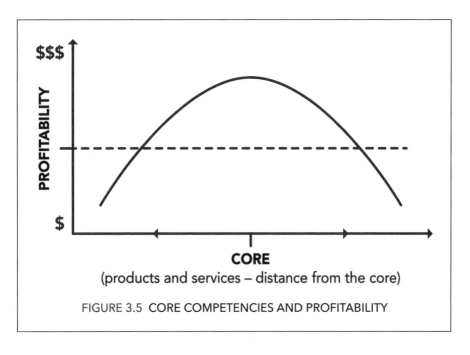

FIGURE 3.5 CORE COMPETENCIES AND PROFITABILITY

Given the difficulty of passing the three core competency tests, we suggest that as an owner-manager you lower your sights and accept a lesser order of perfection. We encourage you to think hard about the first test – being hard to copy – because it is the most important of the three. And if you do, try to look for capabilities that are not a single feature but rather a combination of features that work together to give the advantage. For example, least-cost logistics is a real capability because it works across all distribution and adds value for a customer.

It is one thing to have a competitive advantage but quite another to waste that advantage by having a lousy business model.

What is your business model?

As one owner-manager put it so well, it is important to understand the difference between top-line growth and bottom-line profit. This sounds simple but without the knowledge of competitive advantage that we have uncovered in this chapter a growth plan cannot be written. Having identified that advantage, the trick is to make it work for us in the business model.

Take a biotech firm that has no regular income from trade of any kind. It is not today's customers who are interested in the firm's success; rather it is a future downstream customer and, ultimately, the users of the drugs who will benefit. The party with muscle in the supply chain is the large pharmaceutical company that is keenly watching the biotech firm's research teams at work on the next drug breakthrough, with a view to getting priority rights to it. This understanding of the downstream supply chain offers good insight into an appropriate business model for the biotech firm.

The business model must be a good translation of its competitive advantage.

Once a drug developed by the biotech firm passes the first FDA safety hurdle, the pharmaceutical company will swoop on the firm with a large cash offer so that it can gain advantage over its competitors. Further, milestone payments will be offered for passing the next two stages of efficacy and manufactured product, and finally the pharmaceutical company will offer a royalty on each of the drug products ultimately sold. All this just for being given territorial exclusivity by the biotech firm. The business model is based on lump-sum payments and royalties offered by large distributors for scientifically proven products in return for exclusive territorial selling rights. Whenever we see a manufacturing firm with a high R&D capability, we question whether the R&D actually represents the real jewel in the business – and therefore whether a different business model should be used.

Wine companies have the choice of either going mainstream by selling through large retailers or taking the boutique approach of selling direct from the winery. Scale is needed for the former, and for the latter perceived high quality and lower supply than demand. In the mainstream model, price to the supermarket will drive all the costs incurred upstream and prices will therefore be lower than in the boutique model. In other words, product pricing will reflect the business model.

Whenever we are studying a company we look for the business model to be a good translation of its competitive advantage. After all, what is the point of a business model that doesn't align with the capabilities of the business? In Table 3.1 we have listed a number of business models as a reminder of the wide choice available.

One of the best examples of using your business model to your advantage is the story of Kim and Erica Crawford. They started with the 'advantage' of having no money – and so, nothing to lose. Yet they chose to compete in the wine industry, where having deep pockets is mandatory. Having nothing other than an ability to make wine and a business-savvy partnership, they had others grow grapes for them in Marlborough, contracted winery services for Kim to produce the wine, added Crawford branding and sold it through a Canadian distributor. When the sauvignon blanc proved popular, the distributor became anxious to protect its supply and so bought the brand from the Crawfords for many millions of dollars in consideration of long-term supply to the Canadian market. The strength of this business model lay in producing a high-demand, branded Marlborough wine without the need for significant up-front investment. It was a masterpiece of business modelling.

Today there is significant movement towards businesses undertaking activities that have a 'social good' impact. Such a company might be defined as a social enterprise (SE). The owners of the SE put equal or more importance on the advancement of their good purpose as on

TABLE 3.1 SOME COMMON BUSINESS MODELS

BUSINESS MODEL	HOW IT WORKS	EXAMPLES
Processing/ manufacturing	Raw materials, components assembled into products; emphasis on quality of product and/ or low-cost production	Fisher & Paykel, food processors, electronics, clothing and sports manufacturing
Retail	Goods and services on offer to general public or target niche; sales advertising to attract customers	Any storefront shops, walk-in trade stores, restaurants and cafés
Bait and hook	Sell tool cheaply, hooking user on refills and/or supplies	Razor blades, cleaning products, copiers, printers
Subscription	Sign-on customers for ongoing, monthly fee	Telephone services (except pre-pay), Sky TV, gym/health clubs
Licensing	Intellectual property or technique, tooling allowed by others for fees	'Intel Inside', certified dealers/distributors, Les Mills exercise programmes
Franchising	Whole business systems and processes provided in exchange for fees	Green Acres, McDonald's, Laser Electrical
Tender	Bid against set criteria for lowest price	Construction contracts, transportation providers, health services
Co-operative	Collective of owners, who share processing, marketing and other functions	Fonterra, Zespri, some regional wine grower associations
Primary production	Indistinguishable product, price set by global markets, volume equals yield	Dairy, wool, meat, timber, oil and gas, coal, etc.
Professional services	Charge-up on billable time or set price contract	Lawyers, accountants, IT and IS services
E-business	Provider goes directly to customer via internet and services are often free to customer	Amazon, Trade Me, Google

the earning of profit. Models of social enterprise vary, of course. Here are a few examples:

- A profit-generator model – where a non-profit runs a business and uses the profits to fund their charitable works, e.g. Salvation Army op-shops.
- A trade-off model – a fully commercial operation with a social purpose that compromises the financial returns, such as a work integration model where you exist to employ people with challenges to employment in order to provide training and income and your operation is less commercially efficient as a result, e.g. Kilmarnock (www.kilmarnock.co.nz). A genuine buy-one, give-one model, e.g. Eat My Lunch (www.eatmylunch.nz), also fits in here.
- A lock-step model – where the growth in commercial value is in sync with the social impact.

While combining commercial and social outcomes and responsibilities within one business is admirable and desirable, especially for many young entrepreneurs, it does bring additional challenges. For example, here are some trade-offs that social enterprises face when developing their business model:

- Balancing commercial imperatives with their social/environmental intent – very often there are direct trade-offs between something that costs more or is less lucrative vs. something that will have a bigger social impact.
- Being seen as legitimate on both fronts when society normally separates commerce from direct social outcomes.
- Attracting the right kind of growth capital – philanthropic funding (grants because of the social impact) or debt/equity funding (befitting a commercial operation); or an innovative combination of both.
- Finding evidence that you are genuinely having an impact on a social problem – we're great at doing that with financial outcomes but not so good at understanding social value.

At present, New Zealand only recognises limited liability companies (LLCs) and charitable trusts. The purpose of the latter must be solely 'not for profit' and it is obliged to have an impact on a specific social issue, such as relief of poverty, advancement of education, advancement of religion, or any other matter beneficial to the community. As there is no legal structure in place to facilitate a combined model, several questions will need to be addressed in the future. For instance, should a social enterprise be taxed? If so, at what rate? This conundrum (among others) needs addressing because the demand for social enterprise is increasing and will continue to do so as millennials and future generations enter the workplace.

Planning by venturing into the future

We are making progress. In the previous chapter you determined your purpose and values – or, as Jim Collins, author of *Good to Great*, would say, you now know your core ideology. This chapter has given you guidance regarding financial and business knowledge of your company, being aware of your competitive advantage and knowing how to translate that knowledge into an appropriate business model. We haven't yet covered strategies but these will come once you have a plan of where you want to go.

Before addressing the company plan, we want to remind you that there are several **shorter-term plans** that relate to the ordinary course of a business day, week or month.

Financially, the company will have an annual budget, broken into months according to the seasonal flows of the year. It is always difficult to gauge how challenging to make a budget. Some owners like to stretch their staff with an unlikely budget but this can be demotivating if the staff constantly fail to achieve their targets. In our experience, the best approach is to state your best expectation of what can and should be achieved given outside factors and good management. As the year progresses, it will become clearer whether or not the budget will be achieved, and if an unfavourable variance is expected then a new forecast should be made. There is no point in working to a budget that everyone agrees is out of date.

Other routine plans include such things as capital expenditure, sales and operational plans (S&OPs) to ensure that supplies are on hand when required, DIFOT (delivery in full, on time) to ensure timely customer deliveries, performance management expectations for salaried employees, and staff recruitment plans.

Company planning by imaginatively going into the future has appealed to owner-managers ever since we began running Icehouse programmes. It is a simple process that has real impact. More recently we have added planning for the individual owner-manager, which has added richness and challenge to the process.

Figure 3.6 is a diagram of the planning process.

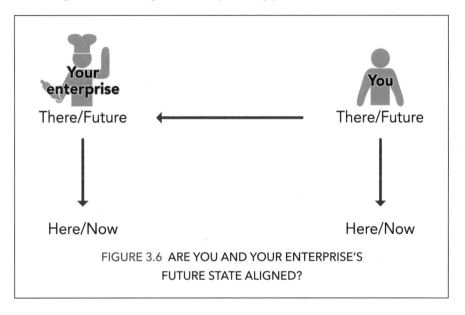

FIGURE 3.6 ARE YOU AND YOUR ENTERPRISE'S
FUTURE STATE ALIGNED?

The planning takes place in two stages, the first for the company and the second for the individual. First, for the company:

- Decide your horizon ('There/Future' in the diagram). Choose a date far enough out that you are not repeating what's happening today but not so far out that you cannot imagine the market environment at that time.
- Let's assume that this is 5 years. Walk out five paces, one for each year.
- Standing in that 'year', record the business environment for your business as you imagine it. Concentrate on what has changed from today.

- Now that you have visualised the environment you will be operating in, describe the best performance you could expect from your company and convert that performance to earnings. Go through a few iterations to make sure you are comfortable with what you have described.
- Now, for the first time, look back to today. Compare the condition of your business at the 5-year point with the business today, and record what you will have to do to get from today to year five. These are your draft strategies for the company.
- Return to today for the business.

Now do the same for the individual (the owner-manager):

- Having completed the position for the company, walk over to the other side and stand in the 'today' position for yourself.
- Walk to the 5-year horizon and consider your environment (family, friends, life). Now describe what you would like to be doing at that point in your life.
- Next, look over to the business at its 5-year point. Do you see yourself in that business? What role do you have? Owner, director, manager?
- Look back to today and record the differences – these are your draft strategies for yourself.
- Now return to today for the individual.

There are two real benefits of this process. First, the idea of going into the future removes you from any present constraints. If you were to plan from the perspective of today, your mind would be full of today's issues, many of which would constrain your ambitions. Issues today are just matters to deal with; you will have many more of them. Second, as the owner-manager, you are forced to judge whether, and in what role, you will retain your interest in the business, all the while considering the extent to which this decision compromises the rest of your life. These are tough but real questions that are often left unasked and unanswered.

The process has application wherever there is diversity in the group, such as a family, a supplier with a customer, partners in a business, a senior management team and its board, or different functions within a company that need to be aligned.

On the face of it, working through this chapter has provided you with a plan, including your company and personal strategies. But strategy is a bigger matter than our brief encounter suggests, and we will have more to say about it in the next chapter. Before we do so, however, there remains one big question to resolve.

What is your company worth?

Most owner-managers won't know the answer to this question and will have little idea of how to go about finding out. However, it makes immense sense that as an owner-manager you know the value of your business. Without doubt it will be the biggest asset in your portfolio, and one day you might be offered what you think is a stunning amount for it only to discover later that it was a steal – for the buyer!

Even more important than knowing the valuation of your business is knowing what drives that valuation, because this gives you clues about what aspects you should be nurturing, what you should be investing in and what you should stop spending money and time on.

We do not claim to be experts on valuation – there is a lot to it. So, rather than holding us to account for every statement, engage a capable valuer and update the valuation annually.

The buyer of a company generally is buying it because that is a better proposition than building their business themselves. They most likely will be a competitor in the same sector, a private equity fund or a high-net-worth individual. A competitor is likely to be bigger, and would be looking to increase market share and reap the synergies that will result from combining the two companies. A private equity fund would gain by driving the earnings of the business very hard for several years before on-selling it. And the high-net-worth individual is likely to be a long-term owner who knows the industry and likes the company.

More important than the valuation of your business is knowing what drives that valuation.

The method of valuation is primarily determined by the condition of the company. In the most common situation, the company will have been around for more than 10 years and will have positive and reliable earnings. In this case the valuation is likely to be a multiple of the future maintainable profits, for which EBITDA (earnings before interest, tax, depreciation and amortisation) is the appropriate proxy. The EBITDA chosen will likely be for the latest financial year but it could be for the current year. Based on the expected sustainability of the earnings, a price to earnings (P/E) multiple is then calculated. This multiple itself is the inverse of the earnings yield (EY), so if a P/E multiple of 5 was chosen then the EY would be 20 per cent. In other words, the buyer would be expecting a rate of return on his or her investment of 20 per cent. If there was confidence that the earnings would grow, then the P/E multiple might be, say, 6, or an EY of 16.67 per cent. In this case a buyer would be prepared to pay a higher price because of the expectation of improving earnings. Of course the opposite holds should the confidence in earnings be lower.

Where the company is much younger and the earnings outlook is less certain, a discounted cash flow (DCF) method might be used. This takes the planned cash flow over, say, 20 years and discounts it at a rate the buyer might require on a risky business and which the seller would be prepared to accept. Owner-managers of smaller or younger companies might be in this group.

Where the company is under pressure and likely making losses, or where the company is attractive for its assets (which might be protected by intellectual property) or large key assets (as in the case of a utility), then valuations will take into account the asset valuation and deduct any outstanding liabilities to give a net worth.

A final word of caution: the valuation of businesses is not a science. We suggest that rather than relying on a public accountant, you instead find a business valuation expert. Have this expert value your business and provide a straightforward explanation of the underlying drivers, so that you can direct your efforts to where the true value lies.

Key lessons:

- Business decisions cannot be made properly without knowing where the money is made and where it isn't.
- Understanding business risk is fundamental. The overriding measure

of risk is the return on investment (ROI). It must sustainably exceed the cost of borrowing funds.

- Know what your company is good at, and translate it into a business model that best exploits that capability financially.
- Planning your company's future from the perspective of that future time, rather than from the perspective of today, will allow you to see more clearly the best opportunities for your company, free from the constraints of today.
- Know what your company is worth. After all, you know the value of your house and most likely the business is worth a great deal more.

4

Strategy

DECIDING HOW TO COMPETE

Businesses cannot function effectively for long without strategy. To not have strategy is to be rudderless, to be a plaything of fate. That said, there are many companies whose strategy is not apparent, yet which seemingly do well. Their risk is that a lack of strategic understanding leaves them exposed to losing everything.

Despite its importance, many people in business struggle with the notion of strategy, so let's start with what it *isn't*:

- It is not an idea. Ideas alone are not sufficiently thought-out to be considered strategy.
- It is not an intention; a desire to do something. Wishes lack the substance of strategy.
- It is not a tactic. That is more tightly focused and near-term – 'Let's offer three for the price of two next week.'
- It is not being the best. While that is what we might want, strategy asks: What should we be the best at, and how should we achieve it?
- It is not a plan. But strategies should be a fundamental component of your plan. We would go so far as to say a plan is hardly a plan if it lacks a strategy.

Harvard Business School academic Michael Porter contrasts strategy with operational effectiveness, which he defines as 'performing similar activities *better* than rivals perform them' – for example, by reducing defects in products or developing products faster. 'In contrast', he says, 'strategic positioning means performing *different* activities from rivals or performing similar activities in *different ways*.' In other words, we can choose how we compete in order to serve a distinct sector of the market. And in doing that, we will differentiate ourselves from the competition in the eyes of the customer.

What is strategy?

In Chapter 3 we talked about core competence. It is from this insight that we begin to decide strategy; strategy is the exploitation of core competence. It is *how* we will win.

Remember the three tests for core competence: hard to copy, easy to replicate, adds value for the customer. Given that these are all difficult hurdles, it is unlikely that your competitors will have the same core competence as you. Even if they have it in the same business functions, it is unlikely that it will involve the same distinct capabilities. Two companies may both be pursuing least-cost operational effectiveness but one might go about achieving that through speed and the other through low-cost inputs. The *how* for each company is different.

Again, to quote Michael Porter, from his article 'What is strategy?' in the November–December 1996 issue of the *Harvard Business Review*: 'A company can outperform rivals only if it can establish a difference that it can preserve. It must deliver greater value to customers or create comparable value at a lower cost, or do both. The arithmetic of superior profitability then follows: delivering greater value allows a company to charge higher average unit prices; greater efficiency results in lower unit costs. . . . Ultimately all differences between companies in cost or price derive from the hundreds of activities required to create, produce, sell, and deliver their products or services, such as calling on customers, assembling final products, and training employees.'

> Strategy is the exploitation of core competence. It is how we will win.

Let's take a look at this in action. Prolife Foods is a Hamilton-based food company that goes to market in two distinct ways. Its packaged products are sold through the traditional grocery category under the Mother Earth brand and as a low-cost offering through the VP (Value Pack) range. Its other format, branded Alison's Pantry, sells fresh nuts, dried fruit and confectionary loose in bins from which the shopper scoops the quantity required into bags. If we look at Michael Porter's graph for strategy differentiation, the distinct positioning of the two categories is evident:

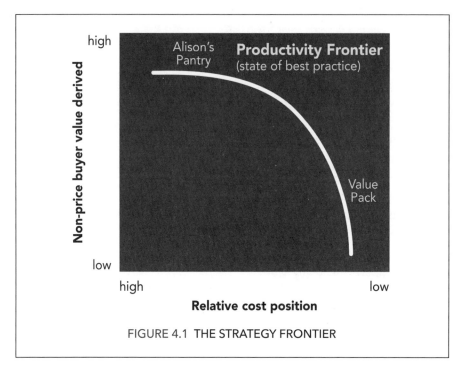

FIGURE 4.1 THE STRATEGY FRONTIER

The barriers to entry for any competitor of Alison's Pantry are high as it takes considerable time to build up skills in the many activities, ranging from overseas sourcing and procurement to the remote management of retail merchandising staff. The advantage this gives Alison's Pantry is further strengthened by supplier and retailer committing to each other on an exclusive basis for this product category. All other offerings of these products are packaged in the grocery aisles. Shoppers' expectation of freshness and their choice of how much or how little to take justifies a higher price relative to pre-packaged competitor products. This is a classic differentiation strategy that yields higher margins for both retailer and producer.

Prolife's VP nut range, on the other hand, is offered pre-packaged in the grocery aisle. The range's low prices and high turnover enabled bulk buying that initially undercut the competition. However, the advantage of least cost could not be preserved. Unlike Alison's Pantry, the offering of packaged low-price nuts was exposed to competition because there was no barrier to entry. First, a reputable trader entered the market with a higher-volume bagged product, then the retailer introduced a house-brand bagged product. Both of these competing products were competitively priced. Prolife's only course of action was to compete on price but with its scale weakened the low-price-point position was compromised and Prolife was forced to settle for a lower market share without differentiation of either product or price.

While Prolife was successful with its differentiation strategy but less successful with its least-cost strategy, the veterinary practice discussed in Chapter 3 was able to exploit its scale position to adopt a least-cost advantage using considerable imagination and execution.

A veterinary business typically competes on a clinic-to-clinic basis, in which commercial products account for approximately 80 per cent of the cost of services to the farmer. A vet clinic could have the best vet–farmer relationships yet lose business because of the cost of products. Addressing this difficulty is not easy because the supply chain is not friendly to vets. Immediately upstream from the vet clinic are the wholesalers for the large international non-human food and pharmaceutical companies with distant head offices near the financial markets of North America and Europe.

Instead of seeing the circumstance as one of David and Goliath, this vet practice set about reversing the odds. It found an ally in a similarly sized vet practice, and over the course of a few years built a scaled-up procurement entity that shifted the procurement transaction from one between a vet clinic and a New Zealand wholesaler to one between an internationally focused vet buying group and a pharmaceutical head office. The new procurement entity became the largest buyer in New Zealand. Cleverly, it set up separate companies to bring in new agency lines and offer them to others in the vet sector, and introduced online selling for all the agency lines, including those similar to their own products. As if that were not enough, it incorporated Australian clinics into its purchasing system and initiated conversations with other international vet groups about doing something similar. This was not lost on the pharmaceutical supply companies, which soon began to offer ex-factory prices that were significantly lower than New Zealand wholesale prices. The result of this highly successful strategy was a shift in earnings from the pharmaceutical company to the international vet buying group and the farmers they ultimately service.

Arriving at strategy

Over many years of reviewing owner-manager business plans, we have distilled a common method for thinking through to strategy itself. We call it 'Arriving at Strategy', and write it as a sequential formula:

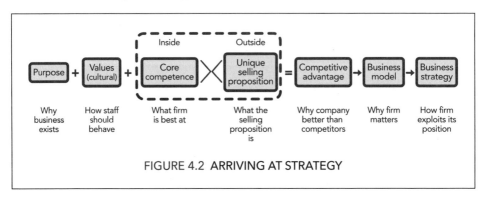

FIGURE 4.2 ARRIVING AT STRATEGY

By now, you will be familiar with all the components of this formula. If we take the example of Alison's Pantry, we can see how the strategy is arrived at:

- Prolife began with an idea, which became a purpose – to provide fresher food with greater convenience.
- The values were built on the owner's belief in always finding a way and never giving up.
- The core competence manifested itself in the Alison's Pantry format. The activities underpinning this included international procurement, the matching of supply and demand, in-store freedom and merchandisers in every store.
- The core competence translated into a unique selling proposition (USP) for freshness and shopper control, which gave Alison's Pantry a differentiated offer that we can call competitive advantage.
- The partnership with the retailer generated a sharing-of-earnings

business model consistent with their combined inputs. Both were well recompensed.

Building on this platform, Prolife was able to introduce activities that further entrenched Alison's Pantry's competitive position:

- The nuts chosen for sale were of the highest grade.
- A wide range of nuts exploited the scale procurement opportunity.
- Third World-country growers were properly remunerated and supported.
- New weighing technology in store included information on health benefits, source of supply and improved control of product sale.
- Considerable flexibility of product offering was made possible by such things as frequent new products, seasonal promotions and news of upcoming events.

These activities are more than marketing tactics. They are coherent, build on the underlying competitive advantages and collectively benefit both shopper and customer.

Blue ocean strategy

In their book *Blue Ocean Strategy*, Chan Kim and Renée Mauborgne wrote: 'to fundamentally shift the strategy canvas of a market you must begin by reorienting your strategic focus from competitors to alternatives and from customers to non-customers of the market'.

Whereas a 'blue ocean' strategy has products positioned away from competitors but in a place highly relevant to customers, 'red ocean' products are hard up against competitors, without advantages and in a setting where they are taken advantage of.

Prolife's packaged goods competitors sit in grocery aisles, completely exposed to the disadvantage of being one of many suppliers struggling to secure favourable terms of trade in a retail market where two retailers have large shares. Alison's Pantry, however, represents a unique in-store proposition. Retailers value this exclusivity and the profit margin it attracts. The result: a rewarding partnership.

Risk and growth

Because the New Zealand domestic market is small, many of our traditional businesses initially seek growth from expansion offshore. However, if the categories such a company focuses on do not have competitive advantage, then the company risks growth for growth's sake – that is, profitless growth. And there is nothing worse. Every day debt mounts, investment costs become losses and the only way forward is to cut prices. These circumstances can be managed if the overall debt position in the company can withstand this earnings and cash downturn. If not, then the company will be in breach of its bank covenants and the bank will increasingly take charge of business decisions.

The lesson here is that expansion initiatives must be properly financed and implemented in categories in which the company has competitive advantage in the overseas market.

During Icehouse planning sessions with owner-managers we often use a risk-management tool to help them recognise where their company is competing:

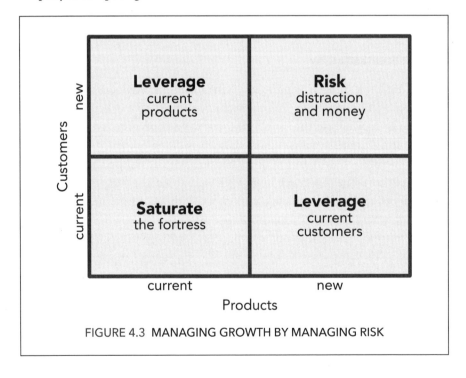

FIGURE 4.3 MANAGING GROWTH BY MANAGING RISK

Strategically, the business should treat current customers and products in the home market as its fortress, with each of them providing leverage opportunities. Current customers are offered new products and current products are offered to new customers, with leverage enabled by reputation. This strategy provides low-risk, predictable growth.

However, when the business elects to invest in a new category, with new products that are to be sold to new customers, the risk increases considerably. The fact that both product and customer are new means that the initiative will get a high priority in the business – a priority that will take the eyes of management off the low-risk initiatives; or, worse, investment in the new initiative will blow out, leaving no discretionary money for the current, safe business.

Risk increases considerably when a business invests in a new category, with new products.

The degree of risk certainly determines impact. Risk is not measured purely in dollar terms but also by the amount of new knowledge embodied in new products or the degree of unfamiliarity with new offshore markets. Cultural differences can also lead to misunderstandings. And manufacturing can become risky if new techniques or processes are used or if the product is contract-manufactured, resulting in a loss of control.

Our experience suggests that, given that a company has a good financial structure, a guide to safety is having 90 per cent in the 'Saturate' and 'Leverage' boxes with 10 per cent in the 'Risk' quadrant – but this is only a guide because there can be many variables at play.

Strategy execution

We often hear that strategy is nine-tenths execution – and while that might be an exaggeration, it is nevertheless true that effective execution is extremely important, as Prolife Foods' expansion into Australia shows.

The owners of Prolife Foods knew that they were onto a winner with the Alison's Pantry range but confidence got the better of them when they acquired a sales company in Melbourne through which to launch the range in Australia. The retailer they were partnered with immediately took advantage of the change of ownership, demanding very tough terms of trade and no time to negotiate. For the next 2 years

Prolife fought, and then retreated. The mistake was to not properly have thought out the execution plan, and to not have sales people with sufficient Prolife know-how to get the job done in Australia.

Some 5 years later, still convinced of the overwhelming advantages of the Alison's Pantry format, the chair and CEO of Prolife met with Coles' head of merchandise. This time the plan was thoroughly worked out; the retailer saw the relevance to its customers and appreciated the advantage it would have over its key competitor, Woolworths. To ensure success, Prolife transferred its New Zealand manager for Alison's Pantry to Melbourne to oversee the execution of the strategy and make sure that Coles understood how to retail the category. The subsequent launch was successful, and today the range, branded 'Scoop and Weigh', is in more than 500 Coles stores. On the back of the successful introduction of Scoop and Weigh, Prolife launched its Mother Earth grocery range in Australia. Today, Prolife's Australian sales are a reflection of excellent strategy and execution.

We should stress that strategy execution is not just a market management role. When it concerns a market as significant as Australia's has become, the company must be reorganised to align the growth with the opportunity. In the case of Prolife this involved three stages:

- The appointment of an Australian manager, supported by a small number of key staff.
- Two-hat management, in which some staff, including the HR manager, CFO and CEO, do two jobs – one for New Zealand and one for Australia.
- Establishing leadership in which Australia is 'service sufficient'.

Such a management structure requires considerable thought, particularly in terms of the timing of changes. Many argue for investing before executing to ensure success, while others argue for investing later to make sure that resources are not wasted. A third group maintains that the two should be concurrent. Whatever path is chosen, being conscious of the question and thinking before acting are essential.

The silent killers of implementation and learning

Much of the success of good strategy execution lies in the competitiveness of a company's products and services, the choice of people to lead and undertake the implementation and their freedom to perform, and the patience and support of the company's leaders.

That said, it is important to understand what typically causes failure so that you can avoid the pitfalls. A study by Michael Beer and Russell Eisenstat, titled 'The silent killers of strategy implementation and learning' and published in the *Sloan Management Review* in 2000, highlighted the following areas of vulnerability:

- Hierarchy or laissez-faire leadership, where top-down, autocratic management or conflict-avoiding discussion undermines required performance. Instead, adopt a leadership style that embraces the paradox of top-down direction and upward influence and welcomes healthy, robust discussion.
- Unclear strategy and conflicting priorities. Instead, the leadership team should develop a statement of strategic priorities which the team commits to.
- An ineffective senior management team. Instead, it must learn to operate as a team by establishing trust, dealing appropriately with conflict, committing to the strategy and accepting individual and collective accountability to get the required results.
- Poor vertical communication. Instead, an honest fact-based dialogue must be established throughout the company.
- Poor communication across the company. Instead, the right people need to work together on the right things, in the right way.
- Inadequate on-the-ground capability. Instead, the people involved must be trained to lead change and drive key initiatives, supported by in-house coaching.

Alignment

To be successful, strategy must 'fit' well and truly into the fabric of the organisation. Strategy is about the combination of activities – the more these activities connect and amplify each other, the more the combination contributes to strategy. An activity cost is lowered because of the way other activities are performed. Similarly, an activity can be enhanced by a company's other activities. In this way, strategic alignment creates competitive advantage and superior profitability. Alignment is a far more central component of competitive advantage than most people realise.

In the case of Prolife's Alison's Pantry brand discussed earlier, the brand's activities combine to give the company a powerful advantage in the market: freshness is enhanced by high stock turnover, quality is guaranteed by using the highest-grade nuts, service is enhanced by in-store merchandisers and so on. Each element reinforces and builds on the others; all are aligned. Imagine how just one misfit – a lower-grade nut, for example – would undermine the rest of the propositions.

Beyond the operational alignment of activities is the question of organisational fit. Earlier, we described aspects of the management appointments that Prolife Foods undertook with its entry into Australia. Alignment occurs if the in-market manager is given the freedom to perform without constant interference from head office. Alignment does *not* occur if head office management insist on knowing the new initiative's daily profit. If that were to happen, the in-market manager would be distracted from what is his or her most important job: successfully establishing the business in the new market. In return for freedom of action, the in-market manager would be expected to always report the truth of the position to head office.

Alignment is a far more central component of competitive advantage than most people realise.

Alignment must occur throughout the company: at the level of operational activities, embedded in management practices and properly recognised in organisational design.

Key lessons:

- All companies, whether large or small, should have a clear, well-communicated strategy.
- Strategy involves knowing what you are good at, and using that capability to serve your customers better than a competitor would.
- Knowing and understanding your strategy enables you to think and

operate your company out of bad times, whether brought on by competitors or by events such as weather and exchange rates that are outside the control of management.

• Thinking and deciding on strategy is a job for the senior people in the company, often supported by an independent adviser, and adopted by the board if the company has one.

• Good strategy, executed well, translates into predictable money.

5

Building the capability of your people

The typical owner-managers we meet are naturally entrepreneurial. They are excellent at identifying opportunities that others don't see and translating these into sought-after market offerings. This opportunistic behaviour not only drives the early stages of many owner-managed businesses, it also sustains them and allows them to compete with much larger corporates. Yet this is only part of the story for businesses wanting to achieve sustainable growth over the long haul. It is essential that owner-managers build organisational capacity, develop people capacity and resource the business for the future, i.e. continue to cultivate future opportunities and ongoing competitive advantage.

We are not saying that any owner-manager should lose his or her entrepreneurial flair – rather, that this behaviour must be combined with disciplined behaviours which together result in new management practices. We term this combination 'disciplined entrepreneurship', which illustrates the importance of combining entrepreneurial flair with disciplined systems and business process, as shown in Figure 5.1.

The management practices resulting from this combination incorporate, in both content and expectation, entrepreneurship activites such as seeking new opportunities, innovation, change and a sense of urgency towards action. The accompanying disciplined behaviours ensure that entrepreneurial flair is organised and managed to achieve a sustainable and future-ready business.

One of the paradoxes that owner-managers face is that you are simultaneously the biggest enabler of *and* potentially the most signifi-

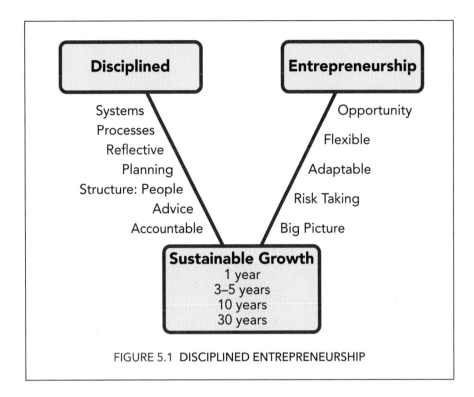

FIGURE 5.1 DISCIPLINED ENTREPRENEURSHIP

cant constraint to the growth of your business. The business extension of this paradox sits at the heart of the challenge to grow – the energy, single-minded determination and excitement that propel initial success can be the very characteristics that limit future growth. In short, what leads to initial success can be the very cause of future failure. In his book *How the Mighty Fall*, Jim Collins explains that this happens when the 'hubris born of success' – leaders losing sight of what made them succeed initially – is followed by the 'undisciplined pursuit of more', with no alignment to core business strengths. Too often, insufficient attention is given to fully resourcing the business so that its full potential can be reached.

Many entrepreneurial owner-managers struggle to develop more formalised organisational structures and processes to enable ongoing sustainable growth.

Our experience suggests that loose, informal, flexible, early-stage business behaviours often persist in organisations as they grow, and that many entrepreneurial owner-managers struggle to develop more formalised organisational structures and processes to enable ongoing sustainable growth. Many of these activities or behaviours fall within a cluster of activities that we call 'resourcing growth' – through people as well as through robust processes, systems and capital. In this chapter we focus on resourcing growth through your people, by ensuring that you have the right people around you in the business.

Growth traps

The potential competitive advantage underpinning many New Zealand owner-manager businesses is that they are not encumbered with rules, regulations, policies and procedures. Things get done quickly, often creatively, and organisational overhead costs do not continue to creep upward and become burdensome.

Conversely, an ineffective structure, lack of clarity around roles and responsibilities, insufficient communication, a poorly functioning senior management team and poor decision-making can severely limit the growth of the business. Without robust systems, processes and structures, the opportunities so easily recognised by New Zealand entrepreneurial businesses are not fully realised, and the potential competitive advantage that comes from size is eroded. From our observations and experiences with entrepreneurial owner-managers, we recognise three common Kiwi management traps that limit business growth:

1. Living in the business

The commonly used phrase of 'working *in* the business, rather than *on* the business' applies here. In the rush of business, you often find yourself on the back foot, reacting to events that you could have anticipated and dealt with proactively. Escaping this trap relies on self-management on the part of the owner-manager in terms of time, energy, prioritisation and organisation. When owner-managers are living in the business, they often fail to find the time to look up and out to see what is happening within their industry and in the broader business environment. This insular perspective frequently leads to resourcing the business to meet the demands of today with little or no consideration of what tomorrow's business will look like, and therefore what resource capability and capacity will be required to meet future needs.

2. Not changing gears

This growth trap typically manifests as owner-managers continuing to get things done the way they always have – which often means relying on themselves. If you hear yourself saying 'It's easier to do it myself' or 'I haven't the time to train anybody else', then you are falling into this trap. There is a tendency to 'do' rather than train and develop others, and a constant feeling of urgency to get things done. Changing gears is all about shifting the focus and cadence of the business: prioritising strategy over day-to-day operations, concentrating on a few key decisions and developing great people to implement the strategy. It is called planning!

3. Not developing people

Loyalty, learning on the job, internal recruitment, non-existent or very informal training and development practices, and being caught up in urgent operational activities can all lead to the trap of poor people management. You may not recognise the capable and willing people within your business. Or you may not think of them as needing coaching, training, or educational or development opportunities to reach their full potential. As a result, they are stifled and your business suffers.

Developing people is harder than it sounds, and often requires specialist advice and input.

You may be thinking 'I care about my people'. And, yes, your heart is probably in the right place but your head may give little thought to practices that enhance the performance of your people. The solution lies in building a culture of achievement and opportunity, aligning people management with business strategy, and providing regular evaluation and feedback of staff performance – including your own. Developing people is harder than it sounds, and often requires specialist advice and input. Additionally, resourcing your business for the future also means stepping back and assessing what skills, experience and capability will be needed to take the business forward, some of which might need to be sourced from elsewhere. Getting the organisational structure right – the right people in the right roles focused on the right priorities – is critical.

EXERCISE 5.1 IDENTIFYING BARRIERS TO GROWTH

Consider the three traps below that might potentially limit the capacity or capability of you and your business, and see which apply to you.

1. Living in the business

a. On average, how many hours per week do you work? _____

b. Rate how productive you would consider your average day to be, on a scale of 1 to 5 where 1 is not at all productive and 5 is very productive. _____

c. Rate your level of outward focus (e.g. exploring what is happening in your industry both domestically and internationally and considering technological, demographic and social trends that might affect your business), on a scale of 1 to 5 where 1 is not at all outward-focused and 5 is very outward-focused. _____

d. After reading Chapter 7, what are some ways to improve your resilience and personal productivity? _____

2. Not changing gears

List three tasks you are currently involved in that ideally should be within the domain of some other person in the organisation. Identify what is stopping you from handing over these tasks.

a. _____
_____

b. _____
_____

c. _____
_____

3. Not developing your people

List your three most important staff members. What training and development (formal and informal) do you have in place for these key people to ensure that they continue to develop their capability?

a. _____
_____

b. _____
_____

c. _____
_____

Building capability and capacity for the future

Recognising the potential pitfalls to growth is one thing, knowing what to do about them and then acting on that knowledge is something else. Frequently, owner-managers tell us they realise that they need to make changes but are not sure where to begin. Here are some suggestions:

Manage and align time and priorities

In his classic book *The 7 Habits of Highly Effective People*, Stephen Covey argues that we could all benefit from considering how we spend our time according to where our tasks and activities sit along two continua: how *urgent* the task/activity is, and how *important* it is (see Figure 5.2). Using the analogy of 'the clock and the compass', Covey asserts that the compass indicates 'true north' based on our vision, direction and overarching goals. These reference points help us determine which activities are priorities and therefore most important. Devoting sufficient time to what is important results in wiser outcomes. By contrast, if our attention is overly focused on scheduled ('clock') tasks and immediate concerns, our decision time gets spent on urgent but not necessarily important matters.

	URGENT	**NOT URGENT**
IMPORTANT	I. (Manage) Crises, pressing problems, deadline-driven projects, last-minute preparation for scheduled activities	II. (Focus) Preparation, planning, new opportunities, strategy, governance, values clarification, relationship-building
NOT IMPORTANT	III. (Reduce) Some interruptions, some calls, some emails, some meetings, responding to some enquiries	IV. (Avoid) Trivial work, junk emails, time-wasters, escape activities, social media

FIGURE 5.2 COVEY'S IMPORTANCE–URGENCY MATRIX

Source: Stephen R. Covey, *The 7 Habits of Highly Effective People*, Simon & Schuster, NY, 1990

Completing your own matrix in terms of the tasks and activities that sit in each of these quadrants often gives valuable insight into where and how you spend your time. Our experience with owner-managers suggests that too much time is spent in Quadrants I and III. For example, do you ever find yourself answering every email, even those about trivial matters, as if they were all urgent, while important matters such as customer relationships, future orders, staff issues and strategic thinking get pushed into the background? How might you be more effective in managing your time and energy so that you are able to focus more on activities in Quadrant II – those that are critically important to the long-term success of the business but are not urgent and are therefore easily deferred?

EXERCISE 5.2 YOUR PERSONAL TASK MATRIX

1. List the activities or tasks that take up your time in each of the four quadrants of the matrix below.
2. Consider what percentage of time during an 'average' month you would spend involved in the tasks/activities within each of the quadrants.

	URGENT	**NOT URGENT**
IMPORTANT	I. (Manage) ___ %	II. (Focus) ___ %
NOT IMPORTANT	III. (Reduce) ___ %	IV. (Avoid) ___ %

Delegate

As a leader, ideally you want to spend as much time and effort as possible addressing issues in Quadrant II of the Covey matrix. To do this, you must effectively delegate to others the tasks that you previously spent time on.

Delegation can be challenging. We have all fallen into the trap of believing that no one is better able than us to do a specific task, manage a particular relationship or make an important decision, and that letting go of this responsibility may lead to a poorer performance or outcome. While this may indeed be true – especially if abdication occurs rather than delegation – such thinking shows a lack of long-term perspective. Without effective delegation, the owner-manager quickly becomes the bottleneck of business growth because progress cannot occur until the decisions and tasks on the owner-manager's desk are completed. And this list of decisions and tasks just gets longer as an organisation grows and becomes more complex.

So, how do you delegate effectively? First, you must establish trust. Delegation without trust becomes a hotbed of frustration as you constantly check, interfere with or override the person to whom you have delegated the task or decision. Sensing the distrust, that person may become immobilised, and ultimately may learn to be even more helpless. Not surprisingly, in this scenario the job will end up back with you – confirming the self-fulfilling prophecy that 'it's just easier to do it myself'.

Successful delegation also requires that you:

- provide sufficient context (the circumstances that brought about the task, why it is important, who else has done it in the past, etc.)
- define expectations (outputs, quality, time, etc.)
- allocate resources (money, people, etc.)
- articulate the review process for progress and completion of the task (i.e. frequent updates or a report at the end of the project).

The point here is that a natural, informal way of managing will often leave the outcome to chance. Worse still, a vague expression of what is expected will leave your management team or employees guessing about what is required, leading to disappointment for everyone. A better approach is to provide guidelines so that both parties have a positive experience.

Delegation is a critical first step in escaping some of the management traps described earlier. It is also the first step towards a culture of both people growth and development *and* accountability.

Manage your people

You may be a 'good people person' but not always good with the people who make money for you. You may be good at all of the tasks that go with managing sales, production, finance, customers and suppliers but not necessarily good at managing the people who make all of these functions happen. The subject of people management fills entire shelves in bookshops but here we offer five mantras that will lift the results of most small businesses:

So, how do you delegate effectively? First, you must establish trust.

1. Take a 'glass half-full' approach

Constantly encourage your staff to achieve more by combining gratitude for a job well done with the possibility of even better outcomes. Believing that people can do more will become a self-fulfilling spiral with many of your key people. Building some 'stretch' into their key performance indicators or expected results is hugely motivating for high-achieving individuals, provided that the stretch is attainable. People are much more likely to offer their discretionary effort (over and above what the job requires) when they work in a positive and enjoyable culture that offers opportunities to grow. Remember, people typically don't leave over dissatisfaction with the actual work they do; they leave because of the company culture and/or their boss. If you want to be an employer of choice, you need to develop and lead a culture where people are motivated to give their best every day.

2. Work where the ground is fertile

Identify high-potential staff and develop them. Opportunities for further growth and development, along with a sense of purpose, are among the characteristics most valued by the next generation of young people coming into your business. Staff with high potential set the standard for others, so create opportunities for them to step up by putting them on interesting projects and providing new challenges. If you see your role as developing future capability and capacity, then supporting and coaching your staff to grow and develop their knowledge, skills and experience is a must.

3. Provide a culture of constant learning

Every staff member must take responsibility for their own development, enabled by the company's practices, and they should know how to improve their capability. Establish partnerships with outside training and development providers who know your business and your expectations. And, importantly, demonstrate a learning culture yourself. It is much easier to engage others when they see you as a role model for constant learning and development. In his book *The E-Myth*, business consultant Michael Gerber argues that too many owners spend time and energy defending what they think they know rather than being driven by an insatiable desire to know more.

> To be an employer of choice, you need to develop a culture where people are motivated to give their best every day.

4. You get what you count

Staff evaluations are a necessary part of the development process. More formal evaluation of performance should not be limited to an annual event; rather, it should be as frequent as both parties think is necessary. Remember, management matters because it enables others around you to be more effective in their roles while allowing you to step back and get perspective. Too often, performance management is considered as something to be done when you are trying to move someone out of the business. In *Outliers*, Malcolm Gladwell argues that for work to be most satisfying, three qualities are needed: autonomy, complexity and a connection between effort and reward. Performance management is not an event but a *process* that involves providing people with feedback (positive as well as areas to improve) and discussing ongoing development opportunities. The aim is to create meaningful and satisfying work that enables people to achieve their potential.

5. Are you really an employer of choice?

Endeavour to keep good staff but don't despair if they leave. Instead, treat their departure as outside training and stay in touch with them; you may employ them again in the future. If, however, you struggle to keep good staff who ostensibly leave to chase a few more dollars with a competitor or to avoid the traffic, it is time for a hard look in the mirror. Most industries are facing labour shortages or skills gaps, and being an employer of choice is a competitive advantage. Some of the most successful businesses we come across are those where people are truly valued, where there is workplace flexibility and an opportunity to grow and develop, and where people come to work because they enjoy it.

If you struggle to keep good staff who ostensibly leave to chase a few more dollars, it is time to look in the mirror.

Understanding the performance and potential of your staff

One useful way to understand the relative performance and potential of your staff is through the Performance–Potential Matrix. This analysis provides the opportunity to consider the positions of your staff within a nine-box matrix based on their current performance and their future potential. Think of it as making valuable use of staff evaluations and development plans. The quality of this subjective task is enhanced by the quality of the evaluation and development process itself, and the assistance of an independent expert or trusted colleague(s). Because it is based on subjective opinion, care is needed to avoid bias and favouritism or to rigidly box people in a manner unhelpful for their future development.

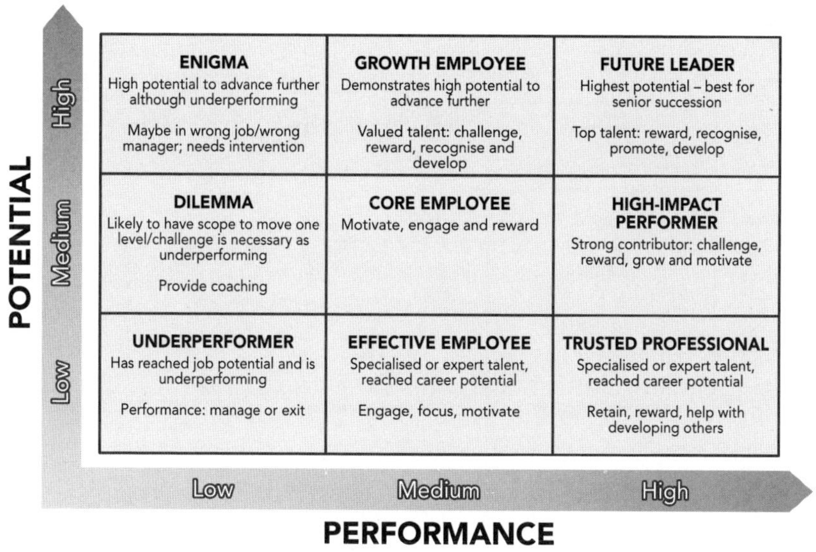

	Low	**Medium**	**High**
High	**ENIGMA** High potential to advance further although underperforming Maybe in wrong job/wrong manager; needs intervention	**GROWTH EMPLOYEE** Demonstrates high potential to advance further Valued talent: challenge, reward, recognise and develop	**FUTURE LEADER** Highest potential – best for senior succession Top talent: reward, recognise, promote, develop
Medium	**DILEMMA** Likely to have scope to move one level/challenge is necessary as underperforming Provide coaching	**CORE EMPLOYEE** Motivate, engage and reward	**HIGH-IMPACT PERFORMER** Strong contributor: challenge, reward, grow and motivate
Low	**UNDERPERFORMER** Has reached job potential and is underperforming Performance: manage or exit	**EFFECTIVE EMPLOYEE** Specialised or expert talent, reached career potential Engage, focus, motivate	**TRUSTED PROFESSIONAL** Specialised or expert talent, reached career potential Retain, reward, help with developing others

POTENTIAL (vertical axis) · **PERFORMANCE** (horizontal axis)

FIGURE 5.3 THE PERFORMANCE-POTENTIAL MATRIX

EXERCISE 5.3 ANALYSING THE PERFORMANCE AND POTENTIAL OF YOUR STAFF

Use the matrix at the top of the following page to assist you with this exercise.

1. Plot your staff within this Performance–Potential Matrix to better understand both their needs and yours. Be careful to avoid bias – ideally, enlist the help of an independent expert or trusted colleague. Check and test your assumptions and what information you are basing your decision on.
2. Consider how that analysis might usefully inform training and development opportunities for various staff members.

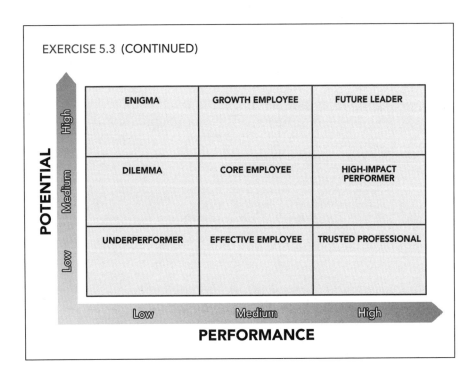

Once the matrix is completed, a picture emerges. It might be that the enterprise has lots of high-performing staff with low potential, resulting in uncertainty about building the company's future capability. Or, the company's poor financial or market performance might be explained by a high proportion of low-performing staff. The 'normal' picture will be one in which many employees are solidly in the middle box, supplemented by a few high-performing expert hands with limited further potential, and other staff with performance gaps but high potential.

The analysis gives the owner-manager the opportunity to provide training and development or to drive stronger accountability regarding performance.

An extension of this analysis is what we describe as testing the 'bench strength' of the company. Drawing on the Performance–Potential Matrix, the owner-manager turns his or her mind to succession issues – particularly those involving senior staff. Clearly, ageing staff in key positions need to be covered by growing the capability of younger staff with high potential.

Developing a high-performing team to cover these challenges and build the capability and capacity for the business to succeed into the future is critical. So, what does it take to organise and manage a high-performing team? Here are some first steps:

1. Start with the premise that you are a team – *not* a number of individual functions but a collective with joint responsibility for the company's goals.
2. Now, work at developing an effective leadership team. Patrick Lencioni, in his book *The Five Dysfunctions of a Team*, captures the attributes of successful teams:
    * Trust – without it, team members won't acknowledge vulnerability.
    * Conflict – without healthy debate, an artificial harmony exists.
    * Commitment – without commitment, ambiguity and apathy drain energy.
    * Accountability – without accountability, lower standards prevail.
    * Results orientation – without outcome expectations, egos and status rule.

    A team in which these behaviours are deeply embedded will be exceptional. Start with these five premises as a way of unlocking the potential in your team.
3. Draw the team together around agreed company values (how we work around here), a business plan (what we agree to do), policies such as hiring, firing, development and remuneration of staff, and practices such as new product development and capital expenditure.
4. Teams benefit from regular contact. Depending on the company's size and the distance between staff, you and your top team should meet (physically or virtually) weekly to communicate what each of you is up to. It might be useful for the team to meet monthly to review results and decide the following month's priorities and resources.
5. Top teams symbolise the health, wellbeing and integrity of the company, so think about yours as a model for the way you want all teams to behave. Excellence without arrogance, commitment to hard work with a sense of humour, and celebration without excess can inspire others to act in a similar way.

When you start to see an important part of your role as developing the capability and capacity of your business to meet future needs, you may be surprised at the way your key managers embrace your vision and begin working together as a true team. Decision-making and performance will improve as people start pulling in the same direction, are better informed about all aspects of the business (not just their functional area) and are more fully engaged in matters of strategic importance.

Having a great team is critical for success but on its own it may not be enough. It can be lonely at the top – which is where a different group of people come in: those who do not work in the business day-to-day but who are available to you for support, input, perspective, advice and wisdom. We call these people 'on call'. They are not on staff but nevertheless are available to you formally or informally as needed. We will explore their role more fully in Chapter 8.

Key lessons:

- Disciplined entrepreneurship is a delicate balancing act between being open to entrepreneurial opportunities and staying flexible, *and* being disciplined in the pursuit of goals and planning.
- Businesses can go stagnant and can fail – developing the right people, processes, systems and information for the future are critical.
- Be aware of growth traps – not investing in yourself and your people creates a ceiling for achieving the growth potential of your business. Challenge yourself and your team to be future-oriented.
- People are a key asset to your business. Spending time building the capability of your team is critical to the future success of your business. As the 'war on talent' (attracting and retaining great people) continues, growing and developing your people can be a competitive advantage.

6

Owner-managers

THE RELUCTANT LEADERS

Leadership is critical if SMEs are to achieve sustainable growth. Yet there is much confusion about what leadership is, why it matters and what kind of leader is most effective. Having witnessed many different leadership styles and types of leaders, what we *do* know is that there is no 'right' approach: effective leadership varies, depending on the situation, and it can be developed.

Many of the owner-managers we encounter could be described as 'reluctant' or 'accidental' leaders. Leadership is not something many of you deliberately seek or give much consideration to. You likely don't even consider that you *are* leaders. This is an interesting point of view, given that, as a group, owner-managers lead businesses that contribute 40 per cent of New Zealand's GNP, employ about 30 per cent of all workers and account for 97 per cent of all businesses!

So, why might being a leader be the last thing on your mind? Perhaps yours is a family business in which leadership was 'inherited'; maybe you started a small business that just happened to grow; or it could be that you still think of yourself as the engineer, the mechanic or the sales person. Hence the term 'accidental leader'. In these examples, being a leader is unlikely to underpin your aspirations and nor are you likely to attribute your business success to your leadership. But if you examine your business, you will see that leadership of some sort does exist. It just may not be the type of leadership that brings out the best in you, your staff or other stakeholders, or the leadership that is necessary for you to achieve future business success. We often hear staff in owner-managed businesses asking for more effective leadership – leadership that inspires them about the future, enables them to grow, develop and fully contribute, and motivates them to go above and beyond what is expected.

Some of you will be natural leaders who effortlessly grow in your leadership role as your business evolves. Others will lead effectively during certain stages of the business's life cycle but less effectively at other times. Get it right, and you can unlock all sorts of untapped potential; get it wrong, and the latent potential in your staff will remain untapped – or, worse, be realised in a competitor's business instead.

Leadership is not management

There is much debate about the differences between leadership and management. In our view, capability and capacity in both are critical for growing a successful Kiwi business. However, one individual may not excel at both leadership and management. Some owner-managers demonstrate excellent managerial skills but are not great leaders. By contrast, some visionary and inspiring leaders are not disciplined and effective managers. Although it is tempting to place higher value on leadership, the reality is that both are critical for business success.

Probably the most useful delineation of the two sets of activities is the time horizon in which they are focused. Recall the horizon thinking we introduced in Chapter 3. The functions of management, outlined in Table 6.1, are behaviours and activities that typically address the needs of Horizon 1 and perhaps Horizon 2; success in Horizons 2 and 3 requires leaders to exercise a different set of behaviours and activities, as shown.

In his book *On Becoming a Leader*, Warren Bennis argues that *management* is largely concerned with resourcing and organising to meet current business challenges. It is focused on controlling processes and solving problems as they arise, and on planning to achieve short- and medium-term goals. It attempts to reduce complexity and ambiguity so the business stays on track to meet its goals. In the previous chapter we explored some of the challenges and opportunities for developing the capability, capacity and managerial skills of your staff and senior leadership team to keep your business on track.

Central to effective leadership is the courage and capacity to initiate change.

TABLE 6.1 DIFFERENCES BETWEEN MANAGEMENT AND LEADERSHIP

MANAGEMENT FUNCTION	LEADERSHIP RESPONSE
Copes with complexity	Produces change
Plans	Sets direction/vision
Administers	Innovates
Organises tasks and staff	Aligns constituents and stakeholders
Controls/problem-solves	Motivates and inspires
Short-range view	Longer-range perspective
Asks *how* and *when*	Asks *what* and *why*
Does things right	Does the right things

Source: Warren Bennis, *On Becoming a Leader*, Perseus Publishing, Cambridge, MA, 2003

Leadership, on the other hand, is focused on the future direction of the business. Central to effective leadership is the courage and capacity to initiate change – including motivating and inspiring stakeholders – in order to achieve the leader's vision. Leaders ask questions about the future and engage others in sharing and achieving their dreams. As Bennis says, they 'keep their eyes on the horizon, not just on the bottom line, and have the capacity to translate vision into reality'.

Bennis does not suggest that leadership is tied to a particular style; rather, it is about achieving future outcomes by engaging in certain behaviours today. There are many ways to successfully lead but they share some underlying principles. At the heart of effective leadership is being true to yourself (*authenticity*), a willingness to recognise your own limitations and strengths (*self-awareness*), a desire to understand others (*empathy*) and a belief that others are capable of excelling (*humility*).

In their book on entrepreneurial leadership, *Leading at the Speed of Growth*, Katherine Catlin and Jana Matthews argue that the role of a leader changes significantly during various stages of growth. These stages require leaders to alter how they focus their time and attention, how they view their role and responsibilities, and which skills and capabilities they draw on. One of the leadership models that resonates most with owner-managers is captured in Figure 6.1.

Typically, the start-up entrepreneur is closely involved in the operational activities of the business, making many decisions every day at the functional, operational and strategic levels. As the business grows, the leader needs to step back by setting the direction, delegating to

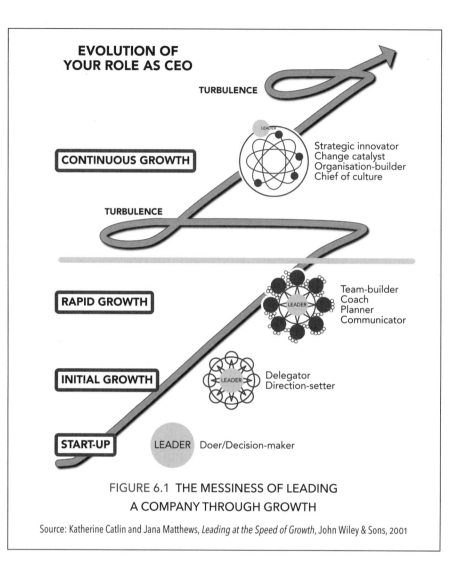

FIGURE 6.1 THE MESSINESS OF LEADING
A COMPANY THROUGH GROWTH

Source: Katherine Catlin and Jana Matthews, *Leading at the Speed of Growth*, John Wiley & Sons, 2001

others and then letting them do their job. During more rapid growth, the leader must rely more heavily on others to get the work done in order to focus on planning for the future, building and developing a trustworthy and capable team, and communicating and coaching people to achieve the goals of the organisation. As the business settles into continuous growth, leadership becomes more strategic. At this stage, the leader needs to engage in activities that build a sustainable and successful culture.

Many owner-managed businesses that are at the stage of rapid or continuous growth still have leadership behaviour that is more appropriate for start-up or initial-growth stages. The leadership style in the founding or early-stage business is typically 'hands on', in which the owner-manager is operationally involved in the day-to-day activities of the business, knows (and is often very loyal to) everyone on staff, has relationships with customers, suppliers and other key stakeholders, makes most of the decisions (tactical as well as strategic) and retains tight control and responsibility for tasks, even if these have supposedly been delegated.

For start-up and early-stage owner-managers, building a senior management team, developing the vision and future strategy of the business, coaching and developing others, and focusing on communication and culture-building are often not priorities. Time and energy are spent on day-to-day activities rather than being invested in the more ambiguous, future-focused activities. It is only as businesses grow, and leaders develop, that they transition from a strongly hands-on leadership style to other forms of leadership.

If you don't change and develop your leadership role over time, your aspirations for business growth may be severely hindered.

Some owner-managers, however, continue to lead their growing business as if it were still small, thereby limiting the potential of the business and the people working in it to grow and develop. This leadership ceiling ultimately stops the business reaching its full potential.

The 'fail-to-scale' syndrome

Leaders must 'look in the mirror' to know their strengths and weaknesses, seeking feedback from their senior team and their employees in general. If you don't change and develop your leadership role over time, your aspirations for business growth may be severely hindered. You may suffer from what leadership expert John Hamm describes as the 'fail-to-scale' syndrome. He argues that many founders 'flounder when trying to grow their businesses because they do not grow their own leadership capabilities to meet the new demands of a bigger organisation'.

Four characteristics can undermine the efforts of entrepreneurs to successfully grow larger organisations:

- **Loyalty to comrades:** Owner-managers can have an over-developed sense of loyalty to their early and/or longstanding employees. Reluctance to address this hard issue can be an Achilles heel for many owner-managers.
- **Task orientation:** Entrepreneurs gain critical momentum early on by focusing on the operational activities of the business; but as the business grows, this behaviour leaves a void in the areas of strategic planning and direction-setting. If your so-called 'board meetings' revert to operational task discussions, you are exhibiting this characteristic.
- **Single-mindedness:** While dogged determination and tunnel vision are wonderful traits in early-stage leaders, over time your leadership view must be more expansive and receptive to the views of others. Sometimes, entrepreneurs do become more open in their thinking but fail to express this shift to others. Both are necessary.
- **Working in isolation:** Leaders need to share their vision, trust others to pursue and achieve it by delegating tasks, and create the right environment for people, otherwise the leader becomes the ceiling on the growth potential of the company.

Leadership development

As stated earlier, we strongly believe that with enough effort, leadership can be learnt and developed over time. Feedback is particularly valuable in this process, although in our experience few owner-managers receive it. Figure 6.2 illustrates a 360-degree leadership model called the Leadership Development Profile developed by Team Management Services. This profile seeks feedback from a variety of stakeholders who work closely with the leader and provides an opportunity for honest feedback across eight important leadership dimensions.

> *We strongly believe that with enough effort, leadership can be learnt and developed over time.*

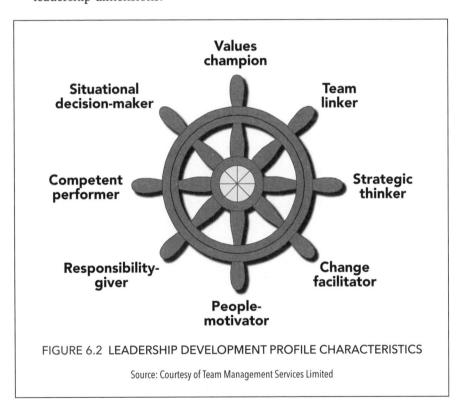

FIGURE 6.2 LEADERSHIP DEVELOPMENT PROFILE CHARACTERISTICS

Source: Courtesy of Team Management Services Limited

Each of these eight dimensions, if embraced and consistently displayed, results in compelling and effective leadership. Briefly, they can be summarised as follows:

- **Values champion:** Lives and promotes the values.
- **Team linker:** Connects work, people, and processes.
- **Strategic thinker:** Develops and progresses a future vision.
- **Change facilitator:** Paces the team through change.
- **People-motivator:** Encourages team and individual performance.
- **Responsibility-giver:** Empowers within clearly defined roles.
- **Competent performer:** Matches personal strengths and effort with what needs doing.
- **Situational decision-maker:** Makes effective decisions contingent on the situation and the people.

When reviewing the leadership feedback of hundreds of owner-managers, we frequently read comments from their staff such as 'This is a great company – tell us your vision for the business so we can help make it happen!' Articulating the direction, goals, aspiration, vision and purpose of your business is a critical first step in getting people to engage in the future of your company. When owner-managers ask their staff to fill out a leadership survey, a significant number of them write comments asking to be given more responsibility, to be trusted, and to be trained and empowered. And they want the owner-manager to be consistent, to share more clearly his or her aspirations and paint a vision for the future.

Given the understated Kiwi way, it is not particularly surprising that owner-managers are seldom forthcoming with praise. As one owner-manager said, 'Of course I don't say "thanks" or "good job". If I don't tell them they are doing a bad job or that something is wrong, then they just know they must be doing a good job.' While this default position may be comfortable for the leader, it does not build a culture that recognises and rewards the commitment and hard work of employees.

Tokens of appreciation need not be expensive or time-consuming. Mystery envelopes, time off for achieving performance goals, hand-written thank-you cards, or gift vouchers for such things as books, movies, beauty treatments, restaurant dinners or ten-pin bowling need not cost much but do send a strong signal of appreciation. Importantly, though, as with any reward system, a clear sense of what is being acknowledged is critical – whether it is hitting a performance target, winning a key customer, completing a significant project or working

EXERCISE 6.2 LEADERSHIP DEVELOPMENT PROFILE

1. Rate your leadership performance in each of the eight dimensions on a scale of 1 to 5, where 1 is 'spend little or no time and effort thinking about or displaying this leadership practice', and 5 is 'spend a great deal of time and effort thinking about or displaying this leadership practice'.

   Values champion _____   People-motivator _____

   Team linker _____   Responsibility-giver _____

   Strategic thinker _____   Competent performer _____

   Change facilitator _____   Situational decision-maker _____

2. What aspects of each of the eight leadership practices are you good at and what could be improved? What actions might you take to improve?

	GOOD AT:	ACTIONS TO IMPROVE:
Values champion		
Team linker		
Strategic thinker		
Change facilitator		
People-motivator		
Responsibility-giver		
Competent performer		
Situational decision-maker		

beyond the call of duty to get a project completed. You don't want to inadvertently reward mediocrity or favouritism.

In *Good to Great*, Jim Collins coined the phrase 'Level 5 leadership'. This describes leaders who bring out the best in those around them. They demonstrate a high degree of respect towards people, are not concerned about protecting their ego and have a strong commitment to achieving results. As such, these leaders exhibit a paradoxical blend of great personal humility alongside professional will and an uncompromising tenacity to succeed. To describe this in action, Collins uses the analogy of windows and mirrors. When things are going well and there have been successes, a Level 5 leader looks out the window first to see and praise those involved in the success. And when something has gone wrong or is not going as well as expected, that same leader will look in the mirror first and ask what they might have done differently, and what they might need to do to improve the situation. This is vastly different from cultures where leaders look to blame others whenever things go wrong.

Emotional literacy

The term emotional intelligence, or EQ, was coined in 1990 by psychologists Peter Salovey and Jack Mayer, who suggested that this form of intelligence was based on the ability of individuals to monitor not only their own emotions and feelings but also the emotional state of the people around them, and to use this understanding to guide their thinking and action. Research has shown that when assessing leaders, more than 80 per cent of the differences between those considered outstanding and those felt to be average performers is linked to emotional intelligence. And importantly, as the leader, your emotions and moods set the tone of the workplace each day.

More than 80 per cent of the differences between leaders considered outstanding and those felt to be average is linked to emotional intelligence.

Your ability to manage and control your emotions has a direct impact on the culture of those around you. As Malcolm Gladwell notes in *The Tipping Point*, emotions are contagious. Effective leaders have highly developed skills in each of the five emotional intelligence domains popularised by psychologist Daniel Goleman, outlined in Table 6.2.

TABLE 6.2 GOLEMAN'S EMOTIONAL INTELLIGENCE DOMAINS

EQ DOMAIN	DEFINITION	HALLMARKS
Self-awareness	Understanding yourself	Self-confidence, realistic self-assessment
Self-regulation	Controlling impulses	Tolerance of ambiguity, integrity
Motivation	Self-starting	Strong drive to achieve, optimism in face of failure
Empathy	Handling people	Understanding, patience, cross-cultural sensitivity
Social skill	Building support	Accepting of others, gains support from others easily

Source: Adapted from Daniel Goleman, 'What Makes a Leader?',
Harvard Business Review, Nov–Dec 1998, p. 95

Rather than emotional intelligence, we prefer the term 'emotional literacy' because we firmly believe that, as with other literacies, emotional intelligence can be learnt. You may know someone who as a youngster was self-centred, insensitive and quick-tempered. Then, when you meet them later in life, they display none of those characteristics but instead have emotional maturity based on self-awareness and a heightened empathy towards others. Their orientation to the world has shifted from themselves to those around them, including colleagues and staff.

Culture matters

As a leader, one of your most critical roles is being 'chief of culture'. Whether you like it or not, you lead the organisational culture. People will look to you to highlight what is valued and what behavioural norms are accepted and expected – regardless of what might be written or said to the contrary. Culture is to your staff what brand is to your customers. Despite this, many companies are willing to invest considerably more time, money and effort in articulating and externally communicating their brand than in defining and internally communicating their culture. Yet, we continue to see businesses that articulate their purpose and vision, live their values and act in a manner that fosters employee engagement and development become highly sought-after employers of choice. Management guru Peter Drucker has said that 'culture eats strategy for breakfast'. In other words, no matter how great a company's strategy and ambition are, success will only be achieved through people.

How engaged and committed your people are reflects the culture of your business. The stories, values, behaviours and practices of you and your staff *are* the culture. In his book *Legacy*, James Kerr offers lessons from the All Blacks. Recent coaches have paid considerable attention to the team culture by developing the highest possible operating standards and expectations, and developing not only the skills of each player but also their character and resilience. 'Collective character is vital to success. Focus on getting the culture right; the results will follow,' Kerr writes. An underlying belief is that performance is the sum of capability and behaviour, with behaviour being defined by values, beliefs and actions of the culture.

> *Culture is to your staff what brand is to your customers.*

As the leader of a growing business you must anticipate transitions and guide and support others through these. You need to hire the right people and use your entrepreneurial strengths to build momentum and bring others with you. Improving your leadership capability will allow you to spend more time on critical growth activities such as opportunity exploration, strategic planning and implementation. Becoming more effective, while keeping your own authentic style, will not only make your role more satisfying and rewarding but will also result in your organisation being better positioned to achieve its growth potential.

Key lessons:

- Leadership is not a choice. As owner-managers you are leaders – even if reluctant ones – and therefore must step up to this challenge. Understanding your leadership strengths and weaknesses is a critical first step to leadership awareness and development.
- As your organisation grows and develops, your leadership must change and evolve. Emotional literacy can improve your effectiveness in almost any situation and with people with diverse backgrounds and experiences.

- Many organisations 'fail to scale' because the owner-manager does not build capability and capacity (their own and that of others) and remains too task-focused, works on today's business not tomorrow's, and is single-minded, or isolated. Culture, purpose and values matter – as the leader you must also be the 'chief of culture', provide clarity of purpose and live the values.

7

Let's talk about you

If you are like most owner-managers, your personal health and well-being often take a back seat to the wellbeing of the business. But without you, there *is* no business. If you are a hands-on manager who becomes unable to stay ahead of the day-to-day activities of the firm, people around you may start to wonder about its viability. Or perhaps you are physically at work but your mind is somewhere else. No one likes working for a withdrawn, frantic or distant leader. Your health and wellbeing can be seen as symbolic of the health of your business. Just as great businesses are built on sound principles and practices, so too is personal wellbeing based on sound principles and simple practices that complement – rather than complicate – your busy schedule.

It makes good business sense to pay attention to your health and wellbeing – life can improve quickly and dramatically if you change a few basic habits such as exercise, diet and sleep. Over time, a few good habits will result in a healthier, more resilient you leading a more sustainable business.

Even if you already enjoy great health, you may still find it useful to refresh and refine your routines so that you can keep them up for the long haul. You may be a highly competitive athlete, or be maintaining a high level of personal fitness for other reasons. If this is the case, then perhaps meditation, relaxation and sleeping are your challenges. Maybe you are so used to constant challenge that you repeatedly swing from boredom to burnout and back. Or perhaps your personal fitness does

This chapter includes material and insights from Dr Sven Hansen, to whom we are extremely grateful.

not extend to your family or to the team at work as you would like it to. Even the physically fit find challenges when it comes to ensuring resilience for themselves and those they care about.

Perhaps the challenge of our uncertain times is to master both our emotions and our thoughts. With the current focus on mental health, we have noticed a significantly increased awareness of the need to understand and discipline emotions and thoughts.

Resilience failure is a very real and predictable consequence of our fast-paced lives and lack of inner balance.

Being an entrepreneur, challenge and pressure is the world you have chosen. As you will see, pressure is engaging and motivating – entrepreneurs thrive on it. What you need is resilience; the learnt ability to bounce, grow, connect and find flow.

Bounce and resilience failure

Bounce is the foundation of recovering from resilience failure, and the first step is understanding and acknowledging resilience failure (see Figure 7.1). If reflecting on this downward spiral is unsettling, well *good*, because it is a very real and predictable consequence of our fast-paced lives when we ignore resilience. Understanding the spiral, its stages and then the steps needed to prevent you sliding down it will enable you to bounce and thus build yourself a more resilient life.

We start by outlining the six stages of resilience failure:

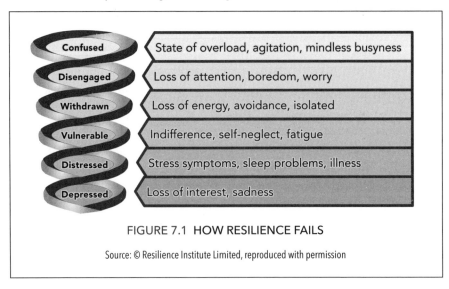

Confused	State of overload, agitation, mindless busyness
Disengaged	Loss of attention, boredom, worry
Withdrawn	Loss of energy, avoidance, isolated
Vulnerable	Indifference, self-neglect, fatigue
Distressed	Stress symptoms, sleep problems, illness
Depressed	Loss of interest, sadness

FIGURE 7.1 **HOW RESILIENCE FAILS**

Source: © Resilience Institute Limited, reproduced with permission

- **Confused (Stage 1: Cognitive risk)**

Mental overload or lack of purpose causes the mind to lose attention. At work, we frequently shift somewhat randomly from one unfinished task to the next, which distracts and confuses us. We begin to worry about what we are not getting done. It exhausts the brain, leading to . . .

- **Disengaged (Stage 2: Cognitive failure)**

In this stage we often find ourselves not paying attention to others. We doodle on paper or daydream. Often we get caught out not listening to someone, or reach the end of a page and realise that we haven't taken in a single word. We are not fully present in our lives.

- **Withdrawn (Stage 3: Emotional risk)**

When not paying attention, it becomes easy to avoid the important but difficult calls, meetings and tasks that need to be done. We begin to lose energy, and avoid contact and engagement with others. Work performance and relationships begin to suffer.

- **Vulnerable (Stage 4: Emotional failure)**

At this stage, we are in a mess: exercise, relaxation and sleep are neglected. We become indifferent to what is happening at work, with family and friends, and in our own life – which is now seriously out of balance. We are a 'sitting duck' for illness, major work errors, relationship break-ups and accidents.

- **Distressed (Stage 5: Physical risk)**

We are now becoming aware that our resources are no longer adequate to the tasks facing us; we feel helpless and out of control. We have trouble sleeping, often imagine the worst and fly into a panic at the smallest of things. The body sends us strong warning signals such as headaches, chest and abdominal complaints, or rashes.

- **Depressed (Stage 6: Collapse)**

Depression is on the increase, with one in five of us suffering from it at some point. Symptoms include a loss of joy, decreased energy, social withdrawal, difficulty sleeping, sadness, self-doubt and low self-esteem. For others this may present as a health crisis.

In Exercise 7.1 we ask you to consider these six stages and reflect on a time when you found yourself heading down the spiral.

EXERCISE 7.1 THE DOWNWARD SPIRAL

1. List the things you do when you find yourself at any of the stages of the spiral.
    Stage 1: Confused _____
    Stage 2: Disengaged _____
    Stage 3: Withdrawn _____
    Stage 4: Vulnerable _____
    Stage 5: Distressed _____
    Stage 6: Depressed _____

2. What do you do to escape the spiral?

    _____

    _____

    _____

So, how do we bounce?

With bounce, post-traumatic growth is more likely than PTSD (post-traumatic stress disorder). When we confront and resolve adversity, we grow in confidence and skill. So, we propose drilling a set of skills at each stage to drive yourself into bounce and back to growth. These skills are practical steps to give you the physical, emotional and mental resources that will allow you to apply the bounce tactics shown in Figure 7.2.

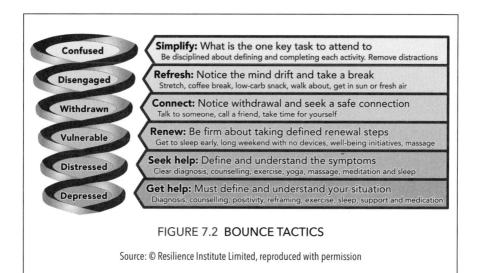

FIGURE 7.2 BOUNCE TACTICS

Source: © Resilience Institute Limited, reproduced with permission

A growth mindset

The popular concept of having a 'growth mindset', proposed by Stanford University psychologist Carol Dweck in her book *Mindset: The New Psychology of Success*, is at the heart of being willing to invest in growing your physical, emotional and mental resources. Just as a muscle or bone becomes stronger with stimulus, so we can significantly grow our emotional and mental strength or fitness. This takes understanding, deliberate practice drills, planning and self-discipline.

The alternative is the 'fixed mindset', which concludes: I am what I am and there is no point in effort; talent, intelligence, social skills and mental fitness are all genetic. This is, first, proven to be a poor understanding of reality and, second, an attitude that will compromise your life and success.

Below we suggest some practices that will contribute to a more resilient you:

1. Take care of your physical wellbeing.
2. Make time for tactical calm.
3. Prioritise family and friends.
4. Build boundaries around technology.
5. Find your 'flow'.

6. Practise the discipline of planning.
7. Enjoy the journey.

This is by no means an exhaustive list, and nor is it in any particular order of priority. Rather, these are suggestions to consider and work with to build a more resilient you.

1. Take care of your physical wellbeing

Monitoring and managing your physical wellbeing is the cornerstone of building resilience. Areas that often need attention include sleep, meal planning and exercise.

Exercise

Current medical guidelines encourage moderate-intensity physical activity at least five days a week. Whatever your preferred exercise, aim for a level of effort equivalent to a brisk walk. Optimal activities include walking, cycling, swimming, tennis, active gardening, house cleaning and kayaking. Even golf is a good start – without the buggy, that is! Choose activities that you enjoy, where there is health value, social interaction (or escape!) and pleasure. Aim for at least 30 minutes per session, but know that even 5 or 10 minutes of more intense activity can secure most of the benefit.

Monitoring and mastering your physical wellbeing is the cornerstone of building resilience.

Make exercise a natural part of your day. One owner-manager started walking every morning for 30 minutes, eventually lengthening that to an hour. Over a period of 5 months he lost about 7 kilograms and needed a new pair of walking shoes. Others have found walking or running at lunchtime a great way to break the day, get exercise and return focused for the afternoon ahead. You know all this. The question is: Are you doing it?

Stretch and strengthen

Stretching should be done by everyone to maintain muscle tone. Basic stretching requires just 5 to 10 minutes each morning. Even though there is very little risk of injury from stretching, it pays to practise good techniques and find a routine that works for you.

Also, pay attention to good posture – in other words, sit up straight. This requires concentration and awareness, which serves as a regular check-in with your body. Refresh your sitting posture, balance your stance and focus on how you use your body to lift, carry and bend. As a quick check, see if you can stand on your left foot for 30 seconds with your eyes closed. Now try the same thing with your right foot. Practise this for a month and you will be impressed by your improvement.

Strength is a poorly understood dimension of physical health. This is largely due to the medical and fitness industries' obsession with aerobic activity. The benefits of increased strength include:

- greater bone density
- better utilisation of glucose, and therefore reduced diabetes risk
- improved sleep, and hence reduced fatigue
- stimulation of the immune system
- stronger tendons and ligaments, and better postural balance
- reduced risk of back and spinal pain.

By following a focused routine you can usually build strength with three 15-minute sessions a week and maintain it with just two 15-minute sessions a week. It is a good idea to discuss this with a qualified fitness trainer and develop a gym- or home-based programme that works for you.

Sleep

Sleep is critical to our ability to recover, regenerate and enjoy the day's activities. Without sleep, the wheels start falling off – we experience reduced concentration and alertness, fatigue, poor decision-making and slow reaction times. About 50 per cent of people experience sleep disturbance and up to half of all workplace accidents are associated with fatigue. In fact, sleep may be the missing link when it comes to physical and mental health, safety and productivity. Most of us need at least 7 hours of sleep a night. Surviving on 4 or 5 hours of sleep a night for any length of time simply doesn't cut it if you want to be at your best.

Taking sleep seriously and establishing a sleep routine is a key aspect of better health. If you are struggling to get a good night's sleep, here are some simple suggestions that might help:

- Learn to notice how your body feels at different times, and make a note of when you start to feel sleepy. If you have a tendency to fall asleep in front of the TV, take note of the time. While 8 p.m. is a little early to go to bed, the chances are that at about 9.30 p.m. you will feel sleepy again. This roughly 90-minute period is your ultradian cycle, and may be the reason why at 9 p.m. or 10 p.m. you might struggle to go to sleep. Or why you feel sluggish when you wake at 6.30, but 6 a.m. works well.

Taking sleep seriously and establishing a sleep routine is a key aspect of better health.

- Get up at the same time each morning, even on the weekends. Experiment to find the right time and then stick with it. If you have a late night, get up at the usual time but take a 'power nap' during the day. A 10- to 20-minute nap after lunch, or later in the afternoon, can head off the problems associated with inadequate sleep – any longer than that and it may be difficult to get going again.
- Prepare for sleep. Try to reduce the amount of coffee and tea you drink after 2 p.m. And remember that alcohol can play havoc with sleep too. Also, think about when you exercise. Sometimes hard physical exercise in the evening can make getting to sleep more difficult. That said, strength training and stretching routines such as yoga can help improve sleep patterns.
- Put yourself to bed and then stay there. If you struggle to fall asleep, some simple breathing techniques can help. Once in bed, lie on your back and relax. Breathe slowly and evenly, focusing on exhalation. Resist thinking, worrying or planning. Maintain quiet, dark and cool surroundings during the night – under 18°C. If you do wake up and have to get up, try not to become fully awake. Do whatever has to be done with the lowest level of consciousness possible and get back into bed. Avoid turning on lights or looking at your phone. Try not to let worry or anxiety take hold – thinking 'now I will never get back to sleep' will not help!

Eat well

No one living in a Western country can avoid the avalanche of information about what to eat. There are books, articles, websites and businesses dedicated to helping us eat right. But running a business means that your days are full and busy, if not hectic, and healthy food is not always the easiest option. If you find it difficult to get out of the office for breaks, or if the local lunch bars serve only stodgy fare, then stock up your office with healthy snacks and fruit to keep you going in the right direction.

One of the success factors in a healthy diet is to 'feed forward' – eat for what you are about to do. With this in mind, here are some guidelines for a healthy and practical diet. In the same way that learning fundamental principles and discipline helps you successfully manage your business, learning how to manage the way you eat, sleep and exercise will unquestionably improve the quality – and quantity – of your life.

So, remember the principles:

• Eat plenty of vegetables and some fruit every day.
• Keep refined sugar and carbohydrates to a minimum.
• Balance your plate with vegetables (fibre and energy), protein (fish, eggs, nuts, meat) and good fats (avocado, fish, nuts, olive oil).
• Plan to enjoy your meals in a pleasant environment with friends.

Avoid fruit juice, carbonated sugar drinks, refined carbohydrates, tropical fruits and overly processed food (meat, bread, sauces, etc.). And treat yourself with avocado, sushi, nuts, dark chocolate (70% plus), blueberries, and richly coloured fruit and vegetables.

2. Make time for tactical calm

We are dangerously overstimulated and subject to the VUCA (volatile, uncertain, complex and ambiguous) world. This has put our sympathetic (reactive) biological system on high alert. This hypervigilant state triggers emotional reactions arising from fear or anger, damages our health, and restricts our focus, creativity and decision-making.

Finding a way to reduce this sympathetic overdrive and allow your parasympathetic (relax and respond) system to kick in is a foundation of success today. Taking time to relax will bring significant benefits, including helping you to be 'present'. Basic relaxation techniques are simple and easy to learn. Aim for 5 minutes to begin with, then lengthen to a duration that suits your day.

Tactical calm tips

1. At first, simply practise breathing out slowly through the nose.
2. Second, take a look at our tactical calm practice below.
3. Third, consider a carefully selected meditation practice and teacher.

Tactical calm practice

1. Lengthen your spine – sit or stand light and long.
2. Inhale gently while paying attention to your belly (see Figure 7.3).
3. Breathe out long and slow (5 seconds) with a slight pause (2 seconds).
4. Inhale low and slow (3 to 5 seconds).
5. Repeat as needed, breathing through your nose.
6. Anchor on a positive state, loved one or goal.
7. Focus attention back onto the drama at hand.

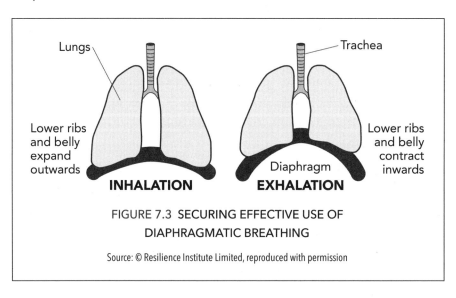

FIGURE 7.3 SECURING EFFECTIVE USE OF DIAPHRAGMATIC BREATHING

Source: © Resilience Institute Limited, reproduced with permission

This relaxation practice can be extended or adapted to a meditation practice. Wonderful resources are now available for this, including online videos and apps, and books written by highly respected professionals involved in the teaching, research and practice of meditation. The objective is to hold your mind calm, stable and alert for 20 to 30 minutes twice a day. However, some research suggests that even a regular 1-minute practice can be effective. So if the challenge of 20 minutes seems impossible, why not take a minute at the start of each hour to breathe, focus and get connected?

3. Prioritise family and friends

When we talk about having a number of balls in the air that we need to juggle, they are often visualised as identical objects such as tennis balls or golf balls. But the reality is that the things in our lives that we juggle – children, travel, exercise, date nights – are not remotely similar and they don't come neatly packaged. Family and friends often take a back seat to the work commitments and obligations that are front of mind. Somehow, we always think that there will be time.

Taking time to relax or meditate will bring significant benefits, including helping you to be 'present'.

A piece of advice that we often hear older owner-managers give to younger ones is to not sacrifice family and friends for the sake of work. Of course this is easier said than done, and we know that our children grow up far too quickly. When it comes to the important people in our lives, it is helpful to think in terms of *quality* of time, rather than quantity of time. Being present and engaged with friends and family for shorter periods is much more enjoyable than spending longer amounts of time stressed-out and on devices. Which leads us to our next suggestion . . .

4. Build boundaries around technology

Information and communication technologies now constitute both a core opportunity and a challenge in contemporary life. Too little connectivity – dropped phone lines, slow internet and so on – is associated with low performance. But too much ('hyper') connectivity can also reduce performance in work teams. A flood of emails, information overload, too many phone calls and too many meaningless meetings can be frustrating; it can also keep us from more important work.

Just like sugar in your diet, there is something you can do about hyperconnectivity. The goal is to find sufficient (requisite) connectivity to be effective, while remaining engaged with the people in your life who matter. Perhaps you can identify with the concept of having just the right amount of connectivity. Maybe you sometimes need to 'just say no' to that phone call or email.

How important is disconnecting? Sven Hansen, author of *Inside-Out: The Practice of Resilience* and a key contributor to our Owner Manager Programme, tells the story of a coaching study that analysed and compared the performance of top tennis players with others who were good but not outstanding. The difference came down to one single factor: what they did between shots. The top tennis players were able to disconnect, shake off every bad shot and move on to the next shot with a clear head. If you keep thinking about the last opportunity or the last conversation instead of clearing your head for the next opportunity, you will not be at your best.

> *The goal is to find sufficient connectivity to be effective, while remaining engaged with the people in your life who matter.*

Having heard about the notion of requisite connectivity and the importance of disconnection, one of our owner-managers decided to try a little experiment. He took his family to the beach one weekend and left his smartphone at home. It was only a short break, but it totally changed the quality of the time the family had together. He had a true break from his business and truly connected with his family. As simple as it sounds, you may want to think about what requisite connectivity is for you and what too much connectivity is. The good news is that we still have some free will, the ability to choose. Choosing to disconnect, even if just for a few moments or days at a time, may be a healthy discipline we all need to practise in the future.

5. Find your 'flow'

The diagram in Figure 7.4 depicts the concept of flow as being one where challenge balances opportunity (utilising existing skill). All too often we talk with owner-managers who struggle to remember a time when they were 'in flow' – where their skills matched the challenge in front of them. For some this is because the challenge seems too massive and everything feels overwhelming, and for others it is due to boredom and the lack of any new challenge.

Note that a new challenge need not be work related. It may arise from taking up a new sport or activity, or re-engaging with something you enjoyed doing but somehow can no longer find the time for.

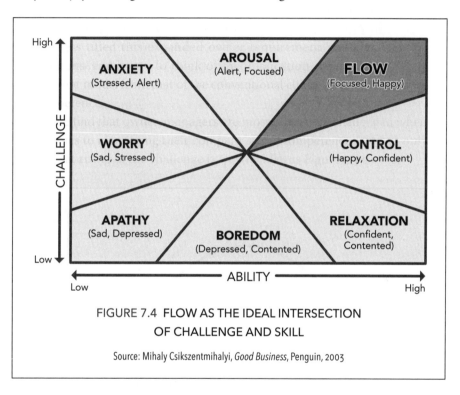

FIGURE 7.4 FLOW AS THE IDEAL INTERSECTION
OF CHALLENGE AND SKILL

Source: Mihaly Csikszentmihalyi, *Good Business*, Penguin, 2003

6. Practise the discipline of planning

As we mentioned in Chapter 5 when discussing *The 7 Habits of Highly Effective People*, urgency and importance are the two reference points when deciding what is most important. We suggested that you complete each quadrant in Exercise 5.2 with your work tasks and activities to shed light on where and how you spend your time. We often get caught in a vicious cycle, captured by the urgent. Answering emails is an easy excuse for you not to have time to visit customers, walk the factory floor, head to the gym or eat a healthy lunch. It is in this mode of operation that we can easily confuse being busy with achieving – but motion must not be mistaken for progress!

Spending sufficient time on the important activities will lead to better outcomes. For successful business growth, the owner-manager must adopt disciplines and activities like those represented in Quadrant II of Figure 5.2. No one other than you has the overarching responsibility for this quadrant. Thinking about the future, deciding priorities, organising to get work done and building good stakeholder relations are the owner-manager's primary job! Note that most of the highly important but non-urgent tasks are for the good of the future. And that often includes your own health and wellbeing. We now suggest that you extend the matrix you constructed in Exercise 5.2 to examine what you do as far as your health and wellbeing 'tasks' are concerned. For example: Is there a health check that needs to be completed? (urgent/important); Does regular exercise need to be part of your weekly routine? (definitely important – is it urgent?). When doing this, it may also help to think about your daily practice. Exercise 7.2 provides a guideline.

Having examined your daily practices, what new goals do you want to achieve? What new habits are you wanting to create to achieve these goals? Put in place a new routine – perhaps starting with one or two small changes and enlisting someone to help you be accountable.

7. Enjoy the journey

We know that 'enjoying the journey' is more easily said than done. But if we keep waiting for the destination – to reach the top of the moun-tain – we may need to remind ourselves that it is a mountain *range*, with another destination looming over the horizon. If we remember to enjoy the journey as well as celebrate our arrival, then not only will our lives be more rewarding but we will also be engaging in a more meaningful way with those we care about.

EXERCISE 7.2 INTEGRAL DAILY PRACTICE

1. Construct a personal health task matrix to identify your personal health and well-being priorities.

	URGENT	NOT URGENT
IMPORTANT	I. (Manage)	II. (Focus)
NOT IMPORTANT	III. (Reduce)	IV. (Avoid)

2. Use the following matrix to help you adopt new daily practices.

BASIC SET-UP	CURRENT	COMMIT-MENT	OPTIMAL
MORNING PRACTICE			
Good sleep (hours)			Aim for 7 to 8 hours of good-quality sleep each night
Wake-up time			Get up at a consistent time each day, even on weekends
Stretching & mindfulness			5 minutes stretching all major muscles, 10 minutes calm, focused breathing
Breakfast			Good breakfast including protein, egg, mushroom, nuts or oats

EXERCISE 7.2 (CONTINUED)

DAYTIME PRACTICE			
Exercise			Aim for 30 minutes daily; include 1 session of strength work per week
Lunch			Veggies, fish or chicken, beans and good fats
Power nap			If you require sleep to boost concentration, aim for a 10-minute power nap
Afternoon snack			Nuts, fruit, avocado and maybe dark chocolate
EVENING PRACTICE			
Switch to home channel			Make a point of disconnecting from work and engaging family
Play time			Have some family or friend time that you can look forward to
Evening meal			Mixed veggies, small amount of protein and enjoy a bit of fat
Sleep preparation			Cool down; avoid screen time at least an hour before bed; engage with family, intimacy or reading
Lights-out practice			Relax your body fully. Engage diaphragmatic breathing, gratitude

Resilience categories	Practical resilience skills
Spirit in Action	Be kind, with wisdom, to others (altruism) Find opportunity to use your skills creatively Build self-confidence and presence
Train Mind	Reframe challenges into opportunities Work hard to be in the present (attention) Notice your thinking (mindfulness)
Engage Emotion	Build constructive emotions (positivity) Develop empathy for others Develop emotional insight and restraint
Energise Body	Clarify your non-negotiables (daily practice) Invest in exercise, strength training, stretching Master sleep and recovery
Master Stress	Learn breath control/tactical calm/meditation Build insight into your biological states Rapid Bounce from adversity

FIGURE 7.5 THE UPWARDS RESILIENCE SPIRAL

Source: © Resilience Institute Limited, reproduced with permission

Summary

The focus of this chapter has been to help you shape a daily practice that can not only support bounce in adversity but also help you grow, connect and find flow – the optimal way to live, work and lead. This is neatly summarised in Figure 7.5.

There is no single, 'right' way but instead many well-researched, safe and effective solutions. Take time to step back, look at your role in your business, consider where you will get maximum leverage, and take deliberate, practical action.

Key lessons:

• Your health and wellbeing is the number one priority for you and your business.
• Review your daily practice – consider what needs to change.
• Experiment with small changes; they can make a big difference.
• Don't be too hard on yourself. Failure provides useful lessons. Pay attention, experiment and never give up.

8

Where to go when you don't know . . .

You may often feel lonely in your business, yet seldom seek advice. This may be because you don't know what you don't know. Your experience and street-smarts can take you so far but they do not prepare you for decisions to do with transition, acquisitions, ownership structures and the like. In this chapter, we discuss the importance of seeking outside perspectives, advice and wisdom. You will come to understand the many circumstances in which you should seek advice and recognise the distinctive roles that tailored outside advice might come from, including mentors, advisers and board members. You need never feel alone again, if you're prepared to seek appropriate advice and support from the best sources available to you.

We begin this chapter with a reminder that at any given time, owner-managers wear one of three hats: 'owner', 'director' or 'manager'. We mention this now because major decisions are often made with your owner or director hat on, and your perspective while wearing either of these can differ greatly from the day-to-day perspective offered by your manager hat.

At least once a year, the owner hat should go on as you reflect on the performance of your key advisers or the independent directors on your board. Wearing this hat gives you an objective perspective along with the backbone to deal with an underperforming director or adviser. Likewise, it enables you to stand alongside fellow shareholders to think about the future of the family business. Even when discussing company performance and plans with staff at the annual meeting, you should wear the owner hat to emphasise that staff cannot take the company for granted; that it has shareholders who require their investment to perform well.

The director hat should be firmly on in a board meeting, where you are equal to your fellow directors. It is the hat that you will be perceived to be wearing when you represent the company to outside parties. And the role brings legal responsibilities that must be remembered.

On-call advisers

As owner-managers you hold a treasure-trove of experience. Some of you have worked in your own enterprise since leaving school, and most of you have experienced the ups and downs of business. You will be very loyal to your staff, especially those who have been with you from the beginning. Typically you work long hours, usually don't like spending money and prefer practical solutions when tackling problems. All of this works well when dealing with familiar situations but in the face of a big and unexpected challenge your knowledge may be thin. In fact, your vast experience may even limit your ability to see the problem or problems ahead of you. In short: sometimes you don't know what you don't know.

Of course not every issue will be major but even small issues benefit from advice. The corporate manager has a floor full of colleagues to 'run things by', from personal assistants to human resource advisers and finance managers. If you have been successful in developing your own management and leadership, you will have a trusted leadership team or a reliable second-in-command who shares your commitment to the business. Your staff will care deeply about solving problems and about continuous improvement. But even if you have that support, and no matter what business you are in or what stage it is at, there will be some issues and concerns that require outside advice.

Such advice comes in many forms, and often changes depending on the age and complexity of the business. We suggest that the people you want to have 'on call' will fall into two camps. First, those that you need to provide knowledge or capability regarding specific questions relating to what is happening in your business. We describe this as 'on-call business capability'. Second, 'on-call advice' relating to the business as a whole. For large businesses this is delivered through some type of governance structure, such as a board of directors. For SMEs the pathway is not as obvious, so we will explore what you might need under the heading 'On-call business advice'.

To set the scene, in Exercise 8.1 consider the issues facing your business at present and how you would normally go about resolving them. We will revisit this at the end of the chapter.

EXERCISE 8.1 YOUR ISSUES

Do you have any fundamental issues that are affecting you and your company?
1. Issues that would benefit from advice or wisdom:
    a. _____
    b. _____
    c. _____
2. What is your normal process for resolving each type of issue listed above?
    a. _____
    b. _____
    c. _____

On-call business capability

No matter how good your team is, it will not be able to provide all the knowledge and expertise you need. For a range of reasons you will experience problems where outside knowledge or capability is required. It might be that you are not big enough to have an HR specialist, or that you are thinking of changing your IT system or expanding your digital reach. Having capability expertise 'on call' at such times makes sense both financially and strategically. HR specialists, for example, can provide expertise for everything from updating job descriptions to managing performance reviews. A number of the firms we work with have harnessed this expertise on a contractual basis – perhaps one day a week, or when a particular issue arises. Similarly, it can be useful to have ready access to IT specialists as needed. Or perhaps you are planning to expand your business and are not sure how to reach a new target market. Again, seeking outside expertise can often save you time and money, and enable you to be more effective in achieving your objective. These examples are by no means an exhaustive list but rather a reminder to continue questioning how best to secure the capability your business needs in order to grow.

An interesting model that we have seen work well is to retain some high-order functional skill while partnering with an outside expert to provide expertise for more troubling problems. This expert's familiarity with the company and its people means that his or her advice can be different as well as pertinent. Being outside the company also allows the expert to assist in evaluating your in-house capability. Such advice is especially relevant for fast-growing companies where capability is constantly being stretched.

No matter how good your team is, it will not be able to provide all the knowledge and expertise that you need.

The fact of it being an outside role also serves as a reminder that your advisers, too, must be growing in their skills; if not, they should be replaced by others able to perform to the necessary level. This is particularly the case when seeking legal and financial advice. Often, owner-managers of companies looking to expand overseas take the risk of relying on the same lawyers and accountants they used when the business was small and operated locally.

The best – or worst – example of this was the case of two Kiwi food innovators who had been working on an invention for 10 years. Finally, they cracked the technology and designed a prototype. It met commercial production-run requirements, and they rightly looked for a multinational to whom they could license their technology. This was done, and the arrangement was signed. Naturally the multinational employed top commercial lawyers, while the two inventors used their provincial family lawyer. In terms of professional service it was David meeting Goliath.

The New Zealand branch of the multinational successfully produced and launched the products but when the overseas head of the multinational began crowing about the global opportunities, the alarmed inventors challenged the multinational, claiming that it had no licence rights outside Australasia. However, an experienced commercial lawyer who was asked to interpret the agreement confirmed that the multinational did indeed have global rights. Ten years of hard slog had been lost at the final hurdle.

These owner-managers knew what they knew – in this case, food processing. But, as their experience shows, it is much harder to deal in matters outside your knowledge base. You must appreciate when you are in a minefield and be conscious of that when seeking help and advice. For serious situations, seek the best technical assistance you can get and remember that many technical solutions also require a commercial understanding to really make them work for you. If you need any further incentive to hire the best, you only have to think about who the bigger companies invariably retain to represent them.

Many technical solutions also require a commercial understanding to really make them work.

In summary:

- Never under-resource a key job. If you have a town-planning problem, get the best planning adviser to fight your case. If it matters enough to you, make sure you win.
- Good partners are better than frequent visitors. Relevant consistency is better for a business than the swinging doors of many different consultants. Partners invest time and expertise and come to understand your business.
- Recognise that you don't know what you don't know. Give outside experts permission to be brutally honest.
- Outside advisers can be a catalyst for change but don't make them the scapegoat or blame them for problems that you created before they arrived.

Mentors

The practice of having a personal trainer is popular today, and is one that staff at all levels appear to value. The owner-manager can benefit from this coaching trend more than most because of the three hats he or she has to wear at different times.

It is important to understand that the role of a mentor differs from that of a company adviser.

It is important to understand that the role of a mentor differs from that of a company adviser. The mentor's advice is directed at the individual – what you should do in a particular case – whereas advice from an adviser is directed at solving a company issue. At times the two roles can become blurred but in essence the mentor will be for the individual first and the company second, whereas the adviser will focus primarily on the company.

Think of the three circles introduced in Chapter 1: 'Your business', 'You in your business' and 'You'. Clearly the adviser connects with the company, and the mentor connects with you. Issues relating to 'You in your business' can involve either, though it is more likely that these will concern behavioural matters that a mentor is more suited to addressing.

None of this is meant to imply that every owner-manager should have a mentor; this is a matter for each individual. But no one will be considered weak for valuing and seeking out such support.

On-call business advice

Despite the constant challenges of running your own business, if you are like most owner-managers you probably do not have trusted, knowledgeable business advisers that you can rely on for wise counsel. As we have noted, you may consult your family accountant, lawyer or banker for technical expertise or for financial resources. And you may bring in specialised advice on HR or IT. But who, other than you, really understands how your whole business fits together? And where can you get independent advice and a different perspective on where your business is today and in what direction it should be heading?

When it comes to the important business issues and decision-making, most owner-managers can feel isolated and lonely. Even if yours is a great business, during the natural course of all business life some serious business matters will arise, such as when:

- you want to step back from full-time management and appoint a CEO
- you receive an offer from a trade competitor to buy your company
- the business is failing
- a long-standing disagreement among family shareholders is coming to a head
- lawyers have presented a very complicated commercial agreement for a supply chain arrangement that you cannot understand
- the business has outgrown the old ways of managing.

You may recognise at least one of these issues in your business. But as an owner-manager, who can you turn to for perspective, advice and wisdom?

Perspective

The difference between an outside and an inside perspective is about four hours. You, the 'insider', wake at 3 a.m. anxious about a problem in your business. Meanwhile, the 'outsider', your adviser, wakes on time for breakfast at 7 a.m. This difference is essentially due to the fact that you live with the issue, while the adviser does not. Understanding and utilising the value of an outside perspective is part of the path towards maturity for an owner-manager. The choice is simple: get some perspective and you'll get some sleep!

Understanding the value of an outside perspective is part of the path towards maturity for an owner-manager.

Living with an issue doesn't necessarily mean that you are dealing with it. The types of issues we are talking about here are the big ones. The ones that sit at the back of your head, unable to get 'air time' because of the busyness of your day. It is only when you get downtime – for instance by taking a holiday – that they float to the front of your mind. These are issues such as:

- My son is not the right person to be running the business.
- How am I going to get Mum to move on from the CEO role?
- I can't see how we are ever going to make money.
- John is just not up to it now but he's been with me from the beginning.

These issues are often crowded out by the crush of today's worries – and today's trivia – but they will not simply go away. It would be convenient if it was just a matter of time – that once you had time you would address the problem but it is more than a lack of time that gets in the way. Being on the inside, you can become captured by the problem. By contrast, the outside observer can often see with clarity what needs to be done.

Often you will think that you are the only person who is aware of the problem. Don't be fooled – your staff not only work with the problem, they also know you are not doing anything about it. Take the example of an underperforming staff member. If you do not act to remedy the situation, you are signalling to your staff that underperformance is acceptable. Your example will influence the standards that others adopt. By contrast, an outside adviser would be black-and-white in matters like that. He or she would give you the resolve to deal with the underperformance.

If yours is a relatively small business operating in a relatively uncomplicated industry environment, then you probably do not need a board of directors. You may not even need an external director. But you might be well served by a trusted and independent adviser who looks at your business, asks good questions, challenges your thinking and perhaps suggests alternative ideas. In this case you get effective perspective but without complications or great expense. And instead of having your mother's accountant as your 'go to' person, why not get a talented engineer or designer to stimulate conversation about next year's innovation rather than last year's tax bill?

Don't get hung up on titles, like 'consultant', 'specialist', 'adviser' or 'director'. What you need around you is *perspective* and *wisdom*, and these come in many forms. You should look for people who have the following:

- **Knowledge:** They must have good knowledge (*know-how*) of your industry and deep knowledge of your business, and you must trust them. It helps if they are well connected (*know-who*), and it is essential that they have good communication skills.
- **Judgement:** Given knowledge and trust, judgement is the blockbuster, because this is when they distil their experience and tailor it to suit your situation. This is where their true value comes into play.
- **Empathy:** Advisers cannot get by with their 'war stories'; they must be with you in spirit, be available and when necessary work at your side. They have to understand your situation, what your firm is capable of and what your people are like. This is no small order but good outside advisers should get *inside* your world willingly, through curiosity and rapport with your staff.
- **Influence:** Often, their key skill is to 'connect' you to the world, or help you 'sell' ideas to other stakeholders; so their access to expertise, and their influence and persuasion, can be as important as their

own knowledge. There have been many intelligent consultants and business mentors that no one listens to.

Clearly, this book cannot prescribe a particular solution for your particular business. However, if you have decided that some form of independent outside advice would be appropriate, you might think about your choice of action as a matter of 'fit' between your firm's stage of growth and the skills necessary to keep moving forward, as shown in Figure 8.1.

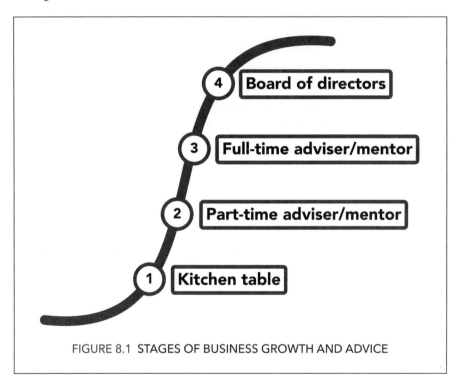

FIGURE 8.1 STAGES OF BUSINESS GROWTH AND ADVICE

The four stages can be outlined as:

- **Stage 1: Kitchen table**
In the beginning, apart from voluntarily sharing with friends and family, it's you and possibly your home partner at the kitchen table.

- **Stage 2: Part-time adviser/mentor**

As the business achieves its first steps – products are sold, customers pay and the early years are worked through – you begin to feel the need to discuss your 'unknowns' with a mentor or adviser.

- **Stage 3: Full-time (regular visits) adviser/director**

Now fully fledged, with responsibilities to other stakeholders, the support of an experienced 'hand' will reassure you as the owner-manager.

- **Stage 4: Board of directors**

Finally, on a larger scale – with perhaps more shareholders, bigger competitors, overseas business, professional management – the owner-manager adopts a regular governance oversight structure in the business.

Board of directors

So far, directors and what they do have been referred to in passing but in this section we will discuss in more depth what they can contribute to your business. Once a company has grown to a certain size, a board of directors is almost mandatory. The board's roles are described below and shown in Figure 8.2:

- **Strategy:** The board decides the firm's strategy and key policies.

- **Resourcing:** The board ensures that the company is resourced to achieve its strategic goals – especially by selecting, evaluating and developing the CEO.

- **Accountability:** The board ensures that it is properly informed on the performance and state of the company, including financial risk.

This model is useful when talking about a more formal governance structure for a business. It simplifies the structure to the three key components: strategy, infrastructure and monitoring. Advisers and directors should assist and guide your business by helping it respond to its environment and markets (strategy), while ensuring that resources

Accountability

FIGURE 8.2 THE DYNAMIC BOARD

Source: Adapted from *The Dynamic Board: Lessons from High-Performing Nonprofits,*
McKinsey and Company, 2003

are committed to the enabling practices that make a business effective (resourcing), and that appropriate financial and risk management is in place and the business is acting ethically and in the best interests of its shareholders and other stakeholders (accountability).

A board in an SME can be more flexible in what it does and how it goes about its work than one in a corporate entity. Figure 8.3 illustrates this point by outlining what boards and managers typically undertake. Think of the diagram as a cylinder containing a moving part, as wide or narrow as you like, that can move up and down the cylinder. It might be that the board chairperson has considerable experience in management, and so is able to train the senior managers in what their management team can undertake in a company. Given that SMEs do not necessarily have these management capabilities, and directors are likely to have been successful managers earlier in their careers, why not use them to assist when appropriate?

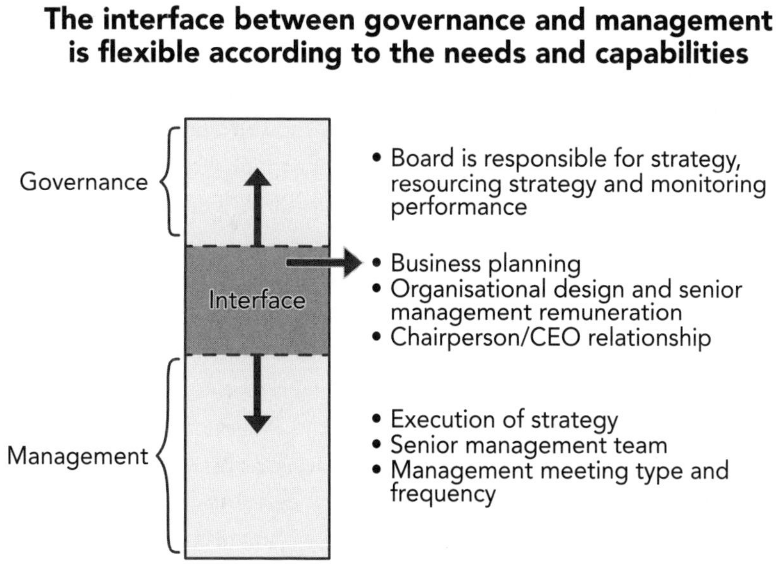

The interface between governance and management is flexible according to the needs and capabilities

Governance $\}$

Interface

Management $\{$

- Board is responsible for strategy, resourcing strategy and monitoring performance

- Business planning
- Organisational design and senior management remuneration
- Chairperson/CEO relationship

- Execution of strategy
- Senior management team
- Management meeting type and frequency

FIGURE 8.3 THE INTERFACE BETWEEN GOVERNANCE AND MANAGEMENT

Flexibility also applies to more routine matters, such as the number of meetings in a year, where they are held and their duration. In corporate life many of these matters are set in stone.

Whatever the nature and form of governance in your business, the basic principles of governance are worth serious consideration, especially as your business grows. All businesses – regardless of size – need plans, adequate financial resources, good people and proper organisation, and all businesses benefit from an independent perspective.

A board can be more flexible in an SME than in a corporate entity.

Here are some observations about aligning wise outside directorial capability within an owner-managed business:

- Directors are inside the tent, advisers are outside. Directors are responsible to the company every day, whether they are physically present or not, and their role imposes legal liabilities. Responsibility to the client is also greater than it is for advisers.

- The chairperson is the most vital of the outsiders you will appoint. He or she must have a deep understanding of your business, build a team of board members, be orientated towards the future not the past and face up to the tough decisions. If they are really important to you, then at the conclusion of their appointment pay them a lump sum according to the benefit they have brought to the company, or give them non-voting shares. It is advisable to seek commercial and legal advice on the arrangement proposed.

- In SMEs the role of directors can be flexible; there is no need to abide by corporate traditions. Directors are usually experienced managers, so make sure you use their know-how.

- Don't hesitate to ask busy people – they are busy because they are capable and like working. Never assume that senior people do not have the time or inclination to work on your business, even if it is relatively small. Let them decide. They certainly won't charge you for the conversation; and if they do say no to your request, they will likely suggest others whom you might approach.

- You don't have to start off by appointing a 'director'. After all, most of us get engaged before we get married. Start off by appointing the person as an 'adviser', and give both of you (say) 6 months to see whether there is benefit to both parties. Then finalise – or terminate – the arrangement.

- Remember that directors are legally liable. You can't just appoint the person as a director and forget about them. They now have rights and obligations to the shareholders and also to the outside world. For example, customers, suppliers and anyone else who relies on the company can sue the directors if it can be reasonably assumed that they should have known about false representations made by a manager or other staff member.

- As with other aspects of capability, recognise that you don't know what you don't know. Give directors and advisers permission to be brutally honest.

- The wise outsider can manifest themselves as a mentor, adviser or director on a regular basis, or as a 'go to' person for a single issue.

- Many owner-managers on our Owner Manager Programme ask where they can find directors and other capable people. Candidates for the position are often sitting in the room with them – other owner-managers. After all, they completely get who an owner-manager is! Another alternative is a recently retired executive from your industry, or even a successful retiree who is the father or mother of a colleague. Failing that, the Institute of Directors or a recruitment company specialising in directorial appointments may be able to assist. But whatever you do, don't appoint your local accountant or lawyer. Apart from the fact that they may not be competent for the job, they certainly will not be independent, which means they will do whatever you ask. And there is not much value in that!

- So, returning to the issues raised in Exercise 8.1, work through Exercise 8.2 below. Be specific about what you need.

EXERCISE 8.2 GETTING ADVICE FOR YOUR ISSUES

1. Write down an important matter that is not progressing.

   _____

2. Describe the adviser competence or skills you would like to assist you.

   _____

   _____

   _____

3. List the names of people you think might best fit your needs.

   _____

   _____

4. If you don't know anyone, how will you find the adviser?

   _____

Succession or transition

The popular term is 'succession' but we think it is best described as a 'transition'. The journey is from 'here' to 'there' – from before the event to after it. Succession places the emphasis on who succeeds whom in the running of the business. In that sense it is a part of transition for the owner, for the staff and for the company itself. For the owner-manager all three hats are up for grabs: ownership, governance and management. The impact on a longstanding owner-manager is very significant.

It is very easy to be drawn into thinking that the price paid or the consideration received for the business is the prize. Of course a good price is a given but there are many other matters that are meaningful to the owner, including the treatment of staff and stakeholders, the attitude and plans of the incoming owner, and the understanding and support of the community.

However, for the owner-manager the first stage to get to is the decision to move on. For many owner-managers this is the biggest change in lifestyle they will ever experience. Most will have spent a lifetime in their business, unlike corporate colleagues who typically change jobs every few years. For owner-managers, the moment of decision is often brought on by a realisation that their capability is not what it used to be, or that there are others who could do the job better. They may have a choice of giving up the management hat and retaining ownership and governance but the next manager will never do things your way, and watching someone else in the role may prove frustrating.

It is a beauty of family enterprises that they can become longstanding inter-generational businesses with an enduring sense of purpose.

This choice of role change for the owner-manager usually only applies where one generation takes over from the other. It is the beauty of family enterprises that they can become longstanding inter-generational businesses with an enduring sense of purpose and values, that employ family members. In New Zealand this is mostly associated with the rural community and inter-generational farming, and with Māori enterprises that have inter-generational ownership through whānau and hapū. For many of these Māori-owned businesses 'the shareholder never dies', and so successful transition to the next generation is imperative.

We think of these family transitions as two 'S' curves – the first being the current generation of management and the second the incoming generation. The two curves are not necessarily joined together; rather, there is a bridge from one to the other, see Figure 8.4. The outgoing owner stands at the top of the first 'S' curve, wishing the transferring staff well as they walk across the bridge to join the journey of the incoming owner-manager who stands at the bottom of the second 'S' curve.

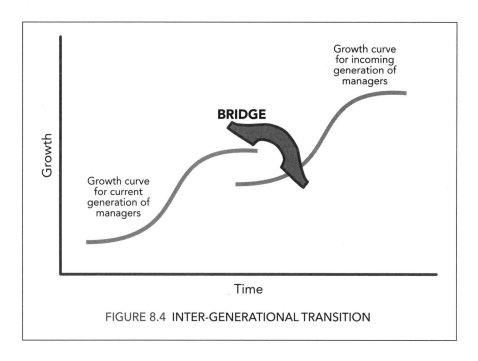

FIGURE 8.4 INTER-GENERATIONAL TRANSITION

The period between one ownership and the next is the transition. In fact, the transition begins the moment the owner decides that it is time to move on. Armed with that decision, the most important thing he or she does next is find a good adviser. Who that should be will differ depending on the size of the transaction. Smaller events are often handled by a business broker, whereas the more sophisticated ones are handled by boutique merger and acquisition (M&A) specialists, by the M&A departments of chartered accountants or, in the case of very large transactions, by the M&A banks themselves. Most SMEs will fall into one of the first two categories.

Getting the right price is vital, of course. No one likes to sell their house below market, let alone a business in which they have invested years of their lives. To get the best price, the company must come to market in peak condition. Reaching that condition may take up to 2 years from the time of the original decision to move on. Peak condition means not only that the earnings must be good but also that there is momentum towards even better results. Valuation of the business will take into account the future maintainable profits; so, while the price paid is based on current earnings, the buyer will agree to a higher multiple if he or she knows that there will be a post-transaction upside to those earnings. All sorts of features beyond the scope of this book will be taken into account to ensure that the business presents itself as 'best in class'.

Securing the right owner for the company is something you will want to do for the sake of your staff, customers and key stakeholders. While it is hard not to simply take the highest offer, 'price achieved' is temporary. What endures is good ownership. It can be gut-wrenching for an outgoing owner-manager to see staff mistreated, to hear customers complain about poor service and quality or, even worse, to see the company fall into a downward spiral for want of good management. So, we encourage you to acknowledge the value of finding a good owner when you are weighing up which offer to accept during the transaction process. Having said that, we understand that there will be owners who, having sold the company, are able to completely divorce themselves from their previous life in it.

To get the best price, the company must come to market in peak condition.

In our opinion, insufficient thought is given to life beyond the sale of the business. What happens to the outgoing owner when they have moved on? Most give it scant thought, with the result that after the hibernation period following the sale, the outgoing owner discovers that golf and travel are not fulfilling enough. Freedom from the demands and expectations of others is great but when people no longer need you, what is your identity? Ideally this should have been thought about during the preparation prior to the sale but usually the owner must go through the sale process before they learn what to do on the other side.

Finding a purpose that is fulfilling will create the magic. This can come from grandchildren or a cause that connects with your values and beliefs. Hobbies and indulgences can also do you good, and there is nothing wrong about having the money from the sale either – it will lead to choices for investment and enjoyment. When it comes to the money though, it is best to retain another financial planning expert to give you wise, independent advice on risk and the like.

This is a time, too, for solace and reflection, which will help you to connect with your inner self. Some people take strengths tests to find out what they are good at, and can be very surprised when they rediscover a capability or characteristic that has lain dormant. All these experiences are healthy. There is nothing wrong with a period of ambiguity.

All owner-managers experience this transition from ownership to their next life. After all that you have done for your business, you owe it to yourself to manage the transition well. So, acknowledge that it will come and that it is better initiated by you than by others, choose a good adviser, plan thoroughly for the business and for yourself, execute confidently and move into your next life fulfilled by your achievement and excited by your future.

Key lessons:

- Recognise that you don't know what you don't know. Without this mindset, you will always be alone.
- The largest gap in SME capability is the lack of an outside, independent, experienced, wise person. Other skill gaps can be covered by experts but the big issues demand support for the owner-manager.
- A board of directors is the ultimate service to owners for the big issues facing the company.
- Succession or transition – whatever it is called – is the single biggest event in the owner-manager's company life. To undertake it without excellent, independent advice is to risk accepting a low price and letting down the staff and customers of the ongoing company.

9

Imagining the future

In Chapter 3 we introduced the Horizons of Growth framework, and we discussed Horizons 1 and 2 in that chapter. Now we turn our gaze to the longer term, beyond the known to the unknown (but important) Horizon 3, to think about the nature of work, business and society in, say, 20 years' time. We will begin with the future of work, in part because it is an area that is being widely discussed as we write this book, but also because the nature of work reflects society and has impacts on how businesses are run.

The future of work

What do we know about the future of work? No one can be certain about what to expect but there are several issues that cause concern.

First, the current rapid uptake and deployment of automation (robots) in the manufacturing and services sectors is expected to continue. Already many millions of jobs are being lost in law, accounting, banking and other professional services as a result of this automation, and millions and millions more robots are on order. Indeed, we have learnt that economies can become or remain strong without significant job creation. Routine jobs, including professional services, are being automated wherever possible. The good news is that non-routine jobs are more difficult to automate, so gardeners, mechanics and baristas may well continue to have decent job prospects.

Second, artificial or machine intelligence, coupled with so-called 'big data', has captured our collective imagination. We see such machines beating humans at sophisticated games and encounter simple applications like 'chatbots' that talk to us in a way that is indistinguishable from human interaction. Natural speech allows us to command home appliances and place orders online, while artificial intelligence can drive cars and trucks, just as planes have been flown with autopilot systems for decades. Third, the Internet of Things (IoT) has brought machines, devices, parts and products online with the result that not just every place but every *thing* on the planet is starting to be networked. For example, tools such as drills and saws can tell us how much work they have done, whether they need a repair, where they have been and who has them now.

These and other advances have raised concerns over data security, privacy and widespread job loss. When everything is on the network, threats to the network can affect almost every aspect of life. While large firms are more likely to be targets of security breaches, small firms are exposed to risks of their own. They may not be able to afford appropriate data security systems, for example; or, even more likely, they may underestimate the risks and so fail to develop human practices, procedures and protocols to protect themselves from such things as data theft, security breaches and extortion.

Jobs themselves will also change, with work becoming more flexible in time, place and space thanks to mobile computing, ubiquitous networks and the power of numerous applications (apps). But this potential is being realised much more slowly than predicted. And while estimates of the number of people working flexibly is high, the reality is that motorways are still choked with so-called knowledge workers struggling to make their way to a cubicle – or maybe a bean bag – in an office building to sit alongside others who have made equally long commutes, when they might have been far more productive working at home. Of course, we do understand that working in the same physical space helps us meet social needs, even if the rational cost of getting there is high.

While we are talking about flexible work, we must also briefly discuss the device that has radically changed not only the nature of work but also many other aspects of modern life: the smartphone. We used to talk about 'work–life balance' but now we talk about 'work–life *integration*'; and in the future we may not even make that distinction as work becomes increasingly embedded into our lives and the occasions that afford us complete separation from work decrease. The idea of coming and going from work may disappear as people have 'gigs' rather than jobs. You may have started your business in your garage but your kids may start their businesses on a job 'platform', where they bid for work, develop a reputation and a brand and possibly collaborate with others from around the globe whom they have never met face-to-face. They may also never own a desktop computer – or a desk, for that matter. Their 'office' will be the kitchen island or the sofa in the lounge, and their IT department will be an app store.

> *In many ways the future is already here, which means that some of these trends may affect you sooner than you realise.*

What does all this mean for your business? Of course, the answer depends on your industry, the nature of your current business, your ambitions for the business and so on. In many ways the future is already here, which means that some of these trends may affect you sooner than you realise. This is all the more reason for you to think about them. While you may enjoy the camaraderie of a shared office space, imagine being able to hire a workforce that required no space, no IT support and no company cars. Think about the possibility of collaborating with suppliers worldwide without spending countless days on aeroplanes. Yes, the Kiwi business rite-of-passage, and the bragging rights that so much flying around the world confers, may come to an end under different economic conditions, or with staff who are less enamoured with travel and want to preserve their personal time as well as the environment.

Gearing up for the future of work means looking at what it will take to find, attract and retain the talent your business requires, perhaps in ways that you haven't thought about. It means hiring a diverse workforce to match our society and to serve the diverse needs of your customers, to whom we will now turn.

What your customers will look like

Work is not the only thing that will change in the future – your customers will change too. For a start, there will be more of them in New Zealand, which is a good thing. However, there will also be more competition both from within and beyond our shores. Only recently did Amazon arrive in Australia and already the retail sector has been rattled. Will your business be shaken or stirred by the increased competition from such a global one-stop shop? Will you be driven to deepen the relationships that have got you where you are today, or will you let price and ease-of-use drive you out of business? Hyper-scale business platforms paradoxically also create opportunities. For example, it took a long time for people to embrace home delivery of groceries but now that Amazon is doing it, every supermarket and corner grocer has seen a growing awareness and adoption of this form of shopping. Moreover, the trust and intimacy associated with being asked to bring home (or send in this case) a loaf of bread and a dozen eggs is an opportunity to forge a new and expanded relationship with that customer.

Do customers want that sort of intimate relationship? Notwithstanding the security and privacy concerns mentioned above, the answer is yes. Most consumers are more than happy to give you access to their home and their data in exchange for reliable, personalised and convenient products or services. What else might customers want? That is hard to say but here is how you can find out. It is no secret that companies that see through the eyes of their customers do better than companies that don't. And we are not just talking about suggestion boxes or customer satisfaction surveys. 'Design thinking' means exploring the deep needs, desires and problems of customers in order to come up with an elegant solution that addresses a problem or fulfils a desire.

Sometimes, customers don't even know that they have a 'problem' until someone comes along with a solution – after which they will no longer tolerate the problem. For example, no one thought that paying for a taxi was a problem until Uber showed us that payment can be done online, not in the car. This is a reminder that there will be a digital aspect to most purchases and practices in almost every sector of business, from health to hamburgers. What will be the changes in your industry?

Sometimes, customers don't even know that they have a 'problem' until someone comes along with a solution.

Do ask your customers what they want – but also consider what they might not ask for but still need and would be willing to pay for. Instead of designing new products and services, you might consider designing and developing a 'platform' (think Uber or Airbnb) on which many products and services can be delivered. The latter is an example of what our colleagues Suvi Nenonen and Kaj Storbacka, in their book *SMASH*, call 'market shaping'.

Market shaping does not totally ignore what customers want or what competitors are doing but its main focus is on creating new ways to inform and lead the market towards a different way of doing things. In a small market like New Zealand, it is easy to get into a rut of following what other markets are doing, or trying to compete on others' terms. Market shaping suggests that markets are not simply a given. They are flexible and malleable, and as such they can evolve and change. Your business may not merely play the game better – it might change the rules of the game. For example, you might stop importing parts and instead print them locally on 3-D printers. Or, instead of building houses in the rain, you might build them inside and erect them on-site when the weather is fine.

> *Your business may not merely play the game better - it might change the rules of the game.*

This may make customers seem a little clueless but they are not. In fact, as New Zealanders become global consumers they have more information and more options available than ever before. Not only will your future customers have opinions but, unlike the polite and understated Kiwi consumer of the past, they will expect to rate, rank and review every product and service, just as – rightly or wrongly – they use such ratings and rankings to form their opinion of your business offerings. Reputation was always important in small-town New Zealand but in the future we are likely to have a 'reputation economy'. So, how are you managing your reputation today? Do you have a social media team – or at least a teenager who keeps you up to date on social media? What about proactively using new media? Whether you are a welder or a wine maker, you could conceivably produce a series of video blogs and become the world's foremost authority on what your business does. This could be even more important if you are in a tiny niche, because when people want to know about that niche, they will discover *you*.

Business author Tom Peters tells the story of the owner of a swimming pool service company in Virginia who decided to make short but helpful videos about swimming pool maintenance. The videos became an instant hit, and rather than being just one of many service companies he became the go-to guy on swimming pools – and of course his company could barely keep up with the demand. Unlike the old days of big-budget advertising, his initiative could be achieved with just a smartphone camera and YouTube.

Remember, people search online for everything, from chicken dinners to chicken diseases and from organ repairs to organic tableware. You may not have thought of what you make or do as 'social', but just as everything will be digital in the future, so every product or service will have a search, social and/or sharing dimension. Are you prepared for a future where word of mouth becomes 'word of mouse'?

Gearing up for the customers of the future means thinking more deeply than ever about their needs and desires. This requires empathy and enquiry but it also involves scanning the horizon for better ways to meet those needs or satisfy those desires. It also means challenging your own assumptions. Many owner-managers swear that their customers want personal, face-to-face service – but while this may be so for pre-millennials, it is far less true for younger customers. Your market will no doubt change, and the challenge is being able to read the faint (and not-so-faint) signals that tell you what customers want or need. It may mean shaping your market rather than just participating in it; rewriting the rules of the game instead of just competing in it.

The new New Zealand

Customer trends in New Zealand will reflect not just new technologies and new social needs and desires but also who we are as a nation. The traditional stereotypical Kiwi who drinks beer, watches rugby and loves cars is giving way to an urbanite who may never own a lawnmower or hold a driver's licence, and who may prefer non-alcoholic beverages. Of course newcomers will play a role but such shifts go beyond immigration – they will be largely driven by your children and by your grandchildren. So, how does your business remain relevant in a world where everyone is both different and changing?

The first major (and largely global) demographic shift that is occurring is towards an ageing population. As a customer base, almost no one has more money to spend than the Baby Boom generation. Moreover, they are more sophisticated ('smart and fussy') customers than their parents' generation, which means that they'll be seeking goods and services of a higher quality and/or customised to their needs or interests. The opportunities are almost endless as this is also the first generation of ageing seniors who are also tech-savvy, meaning that digital services and delivery options are now viable for a large proportion of 'experienced' customers. In fact, there may be a closer alignment between your hard-to-understand millennial employees and your hard-to-understand ageing customer base than you think.

No one knows for sure how things will work out but most agree that more people will also choose to extend their working lives; and many others will have little choice but to remain in employment. In either case, businesses can use this trend to their advantage. Consider this: who could possibly be better at working flexibly at home than a 60-, 70- or 80-something? They would have the discipline, the motivation and the independence to achieve more in a 4-hour day than most others would in a normal 8-hour office setting. And more so if they have come from that office setting, and know all the personalities and the intricacies of getting things done, plus what is expected of them. Of course, they may not want to fight traffic to clock in at 8 a.m. – but that's the point. Why should they? Getting or keeping older workers is not their challenge, but yours. Every time you complain that you can't get good help, look around and think about how you might keep your existing workforce longer, to everyone's advantage.

Getting or keeping older workers is not their challenge, but yours.

The second major demographic shift under way is towards the concentration of the world's population in cities. While the rural-to-urban trend is a global phenomenon, it seems more radical in New Zealand because until recently many of us were still directly or indirectly connected to the countryside. Jaffa jokes are not about Aucklanders per se but the fact that so many traditional towns are losing their kids and neighbours to the 'big smoke'. We are not alone in facing the urban shift of the twenty-first century. As national economies decline in power, cities vie for brand recognition, compete in quality-of-life 'beauty contests' and generally seek to compare favourably with other cities. New Zealand's mystique as a country remains relatively strong, in part due to the *Lord of the Rings* trilogy, sauvignon blanc, dairy products and high-profile sporting success but, as a destination to live and work in, Auckland will continue to extend its economic dominance.

If there seems anything worse for the countryside than people moving to Auckland, it is people moving out of Auckland. As the city's costs of living continue to rise relative to wages, many people are relocating to the provinces. Of course, this demographic shift can be a source of both customers and talent for businesses in provincial towns and cities. A semi-retired accountant may be the perfect addition to your business. They may have big-firm experience but want to work less than full-time, which also makes them both flexible and affordable. The downside for rural and small-town communities is the difficulty of satisfying the needs and preferences of these city folk given a limited resource base and depreciating infrastructure. To take a small example, the prices at your local café are likely to increase when urban-transplant customers arrive with their up-market tastes – although these café customers may also become great customers for your business. The key will be for communities to avoid resentment and instead find ways for these 'outsiders' to be integrated into community life to everyone's benefit.

Which brings us to the third demographic shift: immigration. The New Zealand of the future is being introduced to our country today through work and educational opportunities that attract talent to our shores, some to stay and others who return to their countries of origin with a sense of connection to us. The proportion of immigrants in the population fluctuates, not just because of incoming numbers but also depending on how many of our own young people stay here – as happened during the Global Financial Crisis. The number of Aucklanders born outside the city – more than half – already makes it a 'super-diverse' city but this phenomenon is likely soon to characterise other population centres. For a business, the new face of New Zealand offers challenges in terms of customer preferences and a culturally diverse staff but it also represents tremendous opportunities for businesses that are geared up for the future.

And within this new New Zealand is the resurgence of the Māori economy. Māori enterprises bring together a unique mixture of cultural values, social development and a focus on whānau and hapū workforce development. Culture is also a competitive advantage in establishing and maintaining relationships, brand development and entering new markets, including those on the global stage. As stated earlier, Māori enterprise has a 'shareholder who never dies'. As such, it is not uncommon for strategic planning to encompass anywhere from 150 years (e.g. Ngāti Whātua Ōrākei) to 500 years (e.g. Wakatū, Ngāi Tahu). Again, strategic thinking like this provides an opportunity to engage in a different type of conversation both inside and beyond your business. There is much that can be learnt from engaging with these enterprises.

Building a better world, starting at home

One of the biggest threats to creating a culture of inclusion are the myths we carry with us from the past. Myths are powerful stories that underpin a culture, whether they are true or not. The notion of being a 'classless society', for example, makes it easier for New Zealanders to not take class or status too seriously. However, that myth does not mean that we truly live in a society with no class distinctions. Class is inherent in any culture, and New Zealand is no exception. Moreover, as the gap between the wealthiest and the poorest continues to widen, the notion of social equality becomes harder to sustain.

The myth that New Zealand is a rural nation blinds us to the fact that most of us live in cities. The myth that we are a clean, green, environmentally sustainable nation blinds us to the reality that tourists driving past our eroded hillsides, or encountering beaches and rivers that are not safe to swim in, may see things differently. The philosophical stance of 'exceptionalism' is most commonly associated with the US. But many Kiwis would similarly assert – in their quiet, modest way, of course – that we are the best country on Earth. While nationalism is resurgent worldwide at present, and plays a role in strengthening our collective identity, believing that New Zealand is 'God's own country' and therefore 'as good as it gets' may lead us to feeling superior to others or, worse, keep us from making our country even better in the future.

We have seen examples of proactive shifts in worldviews among our owner-managers. For example, we know of farmers who identify themselves as being in the 'protein' business, whether that protein comes from cows or other sources. We know of veterinarians who advocate a world of zero animal antibiotics, even though such drugs currently make up the majority of their turnover. And we consistently hear concerns about the growth of tourism and its impact on quality of life in places like Queenstown. Indeed, as national tourism numbers surge, we may, as consumers of our own natural beauty, begin the conversation about how special, rare and sustainable that beauty really is.

Building bridges over troubled waters

At present, the world is in a confused state. The global economy appears to be strong, yet is vulnerable as always to shocks and stagnation; the global mood is one of uncertainty, while racism, nationalism, protectionism and other 'isms' have come to dominate the international political scene. The environmental agenda is imposing real economic costs as well as presenting incredible opportunities for small businesses. For example, while 'free range' and 'organic' were once fringe categories, they are now becoming growing market segments with broadening consumer appeal worldwide. Political pressure to buy local is accompanied by consumers demanding to know where their food comes from and the quality, security and sustainability of that food source.

As the owner-manager of a small business in a small country you can hardly change the world – but neither can you afford to ignore global changes. Accepting that you are navigating turbulent waters will make it easier for you and your staff to become more resilient as you prepare for an uncertain future. Your role may be as simple, but pivotal, as hiring new staff without prejudice about what they eat at lunch or when and how they pray. Your role may be to listen to what younger workers, or older workers, or those who are different from you, really want in their workplace. Your challenge is to understand this not as giving concessions to minorities but as future-proofing your business. And it is equally important that you frame your actions in such a way that others in the business understand why such changes are necessary and important for them as co-workers. Despite the vocal views of the few, most people enjoy and celebrate diversity. That is one thing that rural and provincial New Zealand can learn from Auckland.

The environmental agenda is imposing real economic costs as well as presenting incredible opportunities for small businesses.

Framing and re-framing issues is a key leadership skill for an uncertain world. If you see impending doom, so will others. But if you see ways to navigate the uncertainty with positive ideas and initiatives that offer hope to others, you will help shape their sense of what is possible even under challenging circumstances. This is not to suggest a Pollyanna-ish naïveté – far from it. Your challenge is to scan the horizon, not just for threats but also for opportunities and thresholds that will enable your business to continue being successful. Stay connected to industry changes by attending trade shows, and keep up to date with technologies so that new advances don't take you by surprise. If you see drones coming to your industry, don't freak out; instead, become the expert on training drone operators. Embracing all aspects of the future means exposure to bad news as well as good news. But you are the main news source in your business, so think carefully about how you frame the headlines.

Framing and re-framing issues is a key leadership skill for an uncertain world.

How far away is 'the future'?

Where you see yourself in the future depends on how far out you look. If you are just looking into next year, not much may have changed. But if you scan the horizon and detect an upcoming industry upheaval or economic downturn, then you may visualise something more profound. As we discussed in Chapter 4 on strategy, your perspective will change depending on the planning horizon in your sights.

What you see in the world depends on how far away you stand. As shown in Figure 9.1, you and your business are situated within your community (communities) and influenced by technological shifts as well as social and environmental challenges and opportunities.

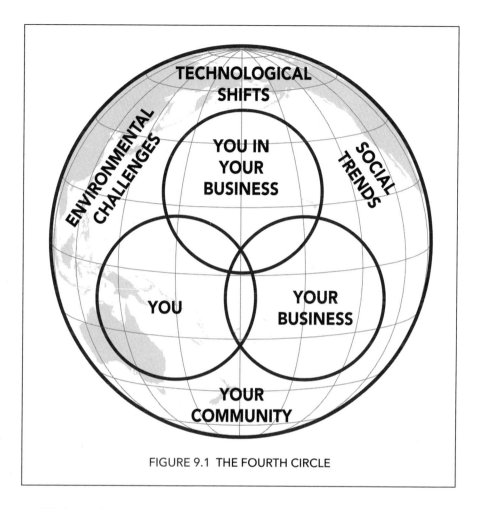

FIGURE 9.1 THE FOURTH CIRCLE

We hope that this chapter has given you something to think about in terms of the near-to-medium horizon. We doubt that we have fully anticipated the longer-term shifts, changes and transformations coming to your particular industry but that does not invalidate the exercise. In fact, we strongly suggest that from time to time you take yourself out of the busy present and ask: What will this industry look like in 20 years or more? And how will the world have changed in that time?

EXERCISE 9.1 GEARING UP FOR THE FUTURE MEANS . . .

For me personally:

_____

_____

_____

For my business:

_____

_____

For me in my business:

_____

_____

_____

Key lessons:

- The future isn't what it used to be. The changes we are seeing now in robotics, automation and machine intelligence will transform work as we know it.
- Technological changes bring social change, which means that many of the challenges of the future will be social, not technical.
- Demographic shifts mean that there is a *new* New Zealand coming.
- Customers often drive change, whether you like it or not.
- Asking good questions and listening well are two of the best ways to keep up with change.

EPILOGUE

WHERE TO FROM HERE?

Where have we come from? Where are we going? As an owner-manager, you may have asked these fundamental questions about your business. More broadly, where are we going as a *nation* of small businesses? What are we 'gearing up' to become?

While size certainly does matter in some industries, scale for scale's sake is not the answer for all. Large or small, our companies have to get better if they are to compete in the next wave of industrialisation – which, paradoxically, will be characterised by the gig economy of self-employed individuals at one end of the spectrum and winner-takes-all world domination by a handful of technology-enabled trading platforms such as Amazon and Alibaba at the other end. Meanwhile, it's likely New Zealand's big players will struggle to remain profitable.

So, what can you do to 'gear up' for the future? Hopefully, through this book you will have found a renewed sense of purpose ('why' you are in business) and some clarity as to which direction you should head in the future. The difference between you and the big firms is that there is less standing in the way of you making your strategy happen. In fact, the only obstacle may be you. As we have made clear, our work with more than a thousand businesses like yours has shown the owner-manager to be both the biggest asset and the biggest liability. Your personal growth and development is critical to your business success.

What makes the difference between thriving and barely surviving is not just skills, but also attitude, perspective and openness to ideas. For you, this will be a lifelong journey of learning. What got you to where you are today won't take you to where you want to be tomorrow. So, we encourage you to keep seeking new perspectives on what you are doing and remain open to what you can or should do differently in the future. This may include taking steps to improve your personal health and wellbeing. The pressures on owner-managers are enormous and the work hours are long. Leading a business can be lonely, so staying connected to your family, friends and community is important no matter what your business goals are.

Once you know the 'why', invariably the 'how' is through the people who work with you – more than technology, marketing or supply chains, they are the most valuable asset you have. If that is not the case in your business today, then you must find the right people and help them to reach their highest potential. In many cases the right people will not look like you, so your job is to attract and relate to others from a range of age groups and with diverse cultural, ethnic and educational backgrounds. If you open to it, you will be 'reverse mentored' by people who are smarter than you or have skills that you lack. To accomplish all this you will need patience, openness and perseverance but your pursuit of excellence will be richly rewarded.

Speaking of excellence, we hope to have put to rest the fading myth of 'number-eight wire' brilliance. While ingenuity and resourcefulness are qualities we should hold on to, just doing what it takes with what we have at hand sells short our ability to do things better. Excellence is a never-ending quest that begins with the next thing you do – whether that is designing a new product or service, writing an internal email or having a conversation with a customer. Your future customers will have grown up in a world of 'insanely great', reasonably priced design, and they will expect nothing less from your organisation. And living on an island 'down under' is no longer an excuse for not delivering.

We New Zealanders have always thought we are different but the recent outbreak of extremist violence in one of our largest cities is just the latest sign that our age of innocence and exceptionalism may be at an end. The same technology that magically allows us to reach out and connect with others across the globe can also breed and spread hate and untruth. You and your business are not immune to the social and technological changes that surround us, nor to the growing responsibility that individuals and businesses have to act courageously in the face of threats to human decency and dignity. You may not have started your business thinking of it as a vessel for social change but given the central role of SMEs in our society, enterprises such as yours will undoubtedly influence the way our communities grow and evolve. Your challenge as a leader is to continually reflect on how you can make a positive impact on those around you, be it as a role model, mentor or leader.

This may seem like a lot to ask of you as business owners but as we pointed out in the introduction to this book, small and medium-sized businesses are the heart and soul of every developed economy. Having worked with a large number of you over many years, we are confident that you are more than capable of gearing up for the challenges that lie ahead. We wish you all the best in your pursuits, and look forward to seeing the results of improved business principles and practices that will benefit you, your family and your community for years to come.

RECOMMENDED READING

Atomic Habits: An Easy & Proven Way to Build Good Habits & Break Bad Ones, James Clear (Avery, 2018). Drawing on research from psychology, biology and neuroscience, Clear presents a simple, easy-to-follow approach to reviewing and changing habits that is applicable to both business and personal challenges. The book includes simple, practical exercises.

Changing Gears: How to Take Your Kiwi Business from the Kitchen Table to the Board Room, David Irving, Darl Kolb, Deborah Shepherd and Christine Woods (Auckland University Press, 2009). Our previous book may not still be in print, but check out your local library or TradeMe for a copy of our original companion text for The Icehouse Owner Manager Programme; it's also available as an ebook. This handbook for small- and medium-sized New Zealand businesses contains case studies that still inspire us and has a slightly different take on issues addressed in *Gearing Up*. We couldn't possibly call it a 'classic', but you might.

Good to Great: Why Some Companies Make the Leap . . . and Others Don't, Jim Collins (HarperCollins, 2001). This is a business classic, filled with expressions that are now in common use, such as 'getting the right people on the bus', 'the hedgehog concept' and 'level 5 leadership'. Collins studied a huge sample of businesses to determine what made the best of them stand out. It turns out not to be flash strategies or fancy organisational gimmicks that help get a company from good to great, but rather a set of enduring principles and practices. Another worthwhile book by Collins and co-author Morten Hansen is *Great by Choice* (HarperCollins, 2011).

Legacy, James Kerr (Constable, 2013). Drawing on lessons from the All Blacks, this book resonates with owner-managers as it explores the secret of high-performing teams and building a culture of success, and asks what legacy will be left behind.

Measure what Matters: OKRs – the Simple Idea that Drives 10x Growth, John Doerr (Penguin Random House, 2018). Doerr, 'a Silicon Valley legend', shares an approach to goal-setting based on OKRs – Objectives and Key Results. Case studies are provided to show

how this approach works. Importantly for us, it was brought to our attention by an owner-manager who is successfully using this in his business. Also, check out Doerr's website (whatmatters.com) and his TED Talk *Why the Secret to Success is Setting the Right Goals.*

'Solitude and Leadership', William Deresiewicz. Originally a lecture delivered to the United States Military Academy, this was published in the journal *The American Scholar* in March 2010. Deresiewicz argues that in a world of over-communication, solitude is what we have least of; yet it is through solitude that we find meaning and a knowledge of ourselves, and discover the value of authenticity.

Start with Why, Simon Sinek (Penguin Putnam, 2009). This book, more than any other, makes the case for why the business is in existence. We capture this vital perspective in the purpose of the company, which is the starting point for writing a business plan. Sinek's *Leaders Eat Last* (Portfolio/Penguin, 2013) has also been enjoyed by some of our owner-managers. It provides a summary of leadership characteristics and practical suggestions for developing them. The book's three key themes of cultivating your 'circle of safety', knowing your 'happy chemicals' and becoming a long-term leader sit at the intersection of the 'You' and 'You in your business' circles.

The 100-Year Life: Living and Working in an Age of Longevity, Lynda Gratton and Andrew Scott (Bloomsbury, 2016). The thought that children born today are expected on average to live beyond 100 years is mind-blowing enough, but understanding what that will do to their work life is revealing and compelling.

The Excellence Dividend: Meeting the Tech Tide with Work that Wows and Jobs that Last, Tom Peters (Vintage Books, 2018). Peters' first book was the 1982 blockbuster *In Search of Excellence*, in which he and co-author Thomas Waterman extolled the virtues of 'management by wandering around' and the power of people to make excellence happen in organisations. His latest book, in his own words, is 'nothing new' – in the sense that he is still fired up about people and culture being the key to any organisation's long-term success. Easy to read and full of pithy quotes (such as 'excellence is the next 5 minutes' and 'amateurs talk about strategy, pros talk about logistics'), this book will inspire you and help you to inspire those around you.

The Second Machine Age: Work, Progress and Prosperity in a Time of Brilliant Technologies, Erik Brynjolfsson and Andrew McAfee (W. W. Norton, 2014). Written by two MIT economists, this is a highly credible, yet accessible, read for anyone wanting to understand the implications of artificial intelligence, robotics and automation on work and society. After a brief history of these technologies, including a discussion of IBM's Watson computer winning at *Jeopardy!* and why robots aren't good at walking down stairs, they make the argument that many more jobs will be lost to technological advancement than will be created. They also explain how and why a universal income policy might actually work. For a shorter version of their work, see their earlier ebook *Race Against the Machine* (Digital Frontier, 2011).

You may also like to check out *The Puzzle of Motivation*, a TED Talk by Dan Pink that explores what motivates people and discusses the importance of autonomy, mastery and purpose.

ABOUT THE AUTHORS

Darl Kolb is professor at the University of Auckland Graduate School of Management. He is currently interested in how we make sense of experience, including new metaphors for a digital age. Darl has been a visiting fellow at the University of Sydney and the University of Cambridge. As an award-winning teacher, Darl leads a core course in the GSM's international Masters of Management programme and serves as an academic facilitator for business growth programmes at The Icehouse.

After a highly successful business career, **David Irving** retired as chief executive officer and area director Australasia, Heinz Wattie in 1997. He was co-founder of The Icehouse Business Growth Centre and has held many governance roles in New Zealand corporate and SMEs including chairman of Prolife Foods for 12 years. In 2014 David co-founded the very successful community leadership development centre in the Waikato, CELF. David has held adjunct and honorary professor appointments at the University of Auckland Business School and currently is adjunct professor in the University of Waikato Management School. He has initiated and served in several philanthropic initiatives. In 2013 David was appointed an Officer of the NZ Order of Merit for his contribution to business and education.

Deborah Shepherd is a senior lecturer in the Management and International Business Department in the Faculty of Business and Economics at the University of Auckland. She currently teaches entrepreneurship, and her research interests are in social entrepreneurship, entrepreneurial mindset and entrepreneurship education. She is part of the directing team for The Icehouse Business Growth Programmes and facilitator on the Owner Manager Programme. Deborah's consultancy work is with SMEs, family businesses and social enterprises. She is a director, advisor or investor in a number of privately owned NZ SMEs and start-ups including her family business Biocell Corporation. She also works with government in an advisory role on SMEs as a member of the Small Business Council and the Australia and New Zealand Electronic Invoicing Board.

Kiwi born and bred, **Christine Woods** is associate professor in entrepreneurship and innovation in the Faculty of Business and Economics at the University of Auckland. Her teaching background is in entrepreneurship at undergraduate and masters level, and Māori entrepreneurship, a component of the Postgraduate Diploma in Business in Māori Development. She is also a life fellow at Clare Hall, Cambridge. Chris is part of the directing team for The Icehouse Business Growth Programmes and facilitator on the Owner Manager Programme. Her consultancy work is with SMEs, family businesses and social enterprises. She is also a founding director of Māori Maps (www.maorimaps.com).

NOTES